RECIPES TO REMEMBER

ALL PROFITS FROM THIS BOOK WILL BE DONATED TO MAGGIE'S.

ISBN 978-1-5272-2898-6

MAGGIE'S CHELTENHAM

RECIPES TO REMEMBER

When we volunteered to take up the idea of creating a cookbook for Maggie's, we were determined to produce something a little different from the vast and growing body of recipe tomes out there. We also wanted to do something relevant to the special nature of Maggie's and, in particular, the amazing emotional support it provides.

The food and memory theme suggested itself almost immediately. From our own personal experiences and from talking to many others, the emotional bond between food and (mostly) fond memories was universal. And when we began to contact people to see if they would contribute their individual stories for *Recipes to Remember* we were delighted and, frankly, overwhelmed by the response.

In the following pages, you'll find memories and associated recipes donated by who we are proud to call 'All Kinds of People'. Some names you may know, some you won't. Their stories can be funny, moving, intriguing and insightful — sometimes all four. The recipes themselves are equally varied, ranging from the precisely detailed to the gloriously rough and ready.

However, emerging through all this wonderful variety (and the irresistible glimpses into other people's lives) is the reassuring feeling that us humans have much more in common than we might sometimes think. And when it comes to food, memory and the often heartfelt connection between them — we're probably all on the same page.

KELLY & TASH

WHAT IS IT ABOUT
FOOD AND MEMORY?

They seem like natural partners — made for each other and as inseparable as sticky rice and deep pile tufted rug (long story). But why are they so tightly linked together?

Well, for a start, nobody can deny that food is pretty fundamental to our survival — preferably along with regular supplies of air, water and shelter. That means our brains are likely to be chock-full of food-related content. Hopefully, there's a little room left for other stuff but who really knows?

Then there's the sensory thing. For the fortunate who are able to move beyond the "Where is my next meal coming from?" stage, food can tick every one of the sensation boxes as easily as falling off a chocolate log. Sight, smell, taste, touch, and even hearing (don't forget the sizzle and snap), all get a concentrated work-out when food is on the menu.

Furthermore, the experts tell us that when these food-related sensations are encountered together (assisted by a tasty toad in the hole, say, or a succulent strawberry sponge — choose your own example), they establish strong patterns of connections in the brain that form memories.

But the ability of our food experiences to lay down memories is enhanced even more by the circumstances and especially the human connections we associate with those experiences. And that's why a certain dish, or even the merest hint of its aroma, is enough to transport us instantly to a particular time or place and to remind us of those who shared it with us. Forget time travel — try a cheese and pickle sandwich.

CONTENTS

TO ENSURE RESULTS ARE AS RELIABLE
AS POSSIBLE, WE HAVE REPRODUCED THE
FOLLOWING RECIPES EXACTLY AS PROVIDED
BY OUR CONTRIBUTORS.

YOU MAY WISH TO CONVERT SOME WEIGHTS,
MEASURES AND COOKING TEMPERATURES TO
YOUR PREFERRED UNITS.

SAVOURY

IAIN & ERNIE GIRDLESTONE
Husband, Father and Cook

When our eldest son Ernie was 2 and a bit we found ourselves in a wine bar somewhere in Gloucestershire. We were with a French friend who insisted it was normal to carry a toddler into these places. Ernie decided to order some snacks from behind the bar which cost about £6 each and came served in a thimble. He decided he liked the spicy mixed nuts most of all.

Some weeks later we were in a well-known high street supermarket scanning the snack aisle when Ernie piped up that we should get some "nuts like we had in the wine bar". I grabbed some spicy cashews and scarpered while a cluster of pensioners laughed at us.

To cut a long story short, the shop nuts were pretty awful, so we made our own.

ERNIE'S NUTS FROM THE WINE BAR

Ingredients

300g CASHEW NUTS.

300g PECANS (both unsalted and not roasted).

75g SUNFLOWER SEEDS.

40g SESAME SEEDS.

40g DESICCATED COCONUT.

ZEST of LARGE ORANGE.

ZEST of a LEMON.

ZEST of a LIME.

50g SOFT BROWN SUGAR.

15g of FAJITA SPICE MIX.

1 tsp SEA SALT.

2 EGG WHITES.

1 tbsp RUNNY HONEY.

Method

Preheat oven to 160°C and line a large flat baking tray with good quality baking parchment.

Beat the egg whites and sugar till soft peaks. Add the fajita, salt and zests. Mix well, then fold in all nuts (including the coconut) and seeds.

Pour onto a tray and spread out. Then bake for about 15 mins until starting to brown.

Take out and add the honey. I pour back into the original bowl to get an even coating but you could do this on the tray.

Return to the oven and repeat baking and mixing every 5 minutes until you achieve an even golden-brown colour. This could take a total of about 30 mins depending on your oven.

MARIA PASCOE
Maggie's Cheltenham Fundraiser

Pebre always brings back memories of both my childhood as a Chilean exile child growing up in Swansea, but also my time in Chile when I returned as a teenager.

I was brought up in a very Chilean home, where my parents felt it very important to never lose my roots and traditions. They were always grateful for the opportunities life had given them, despite the enormous difficulties and challenges they faced along the way as immigrants in the UK. Despite this, I always remember a sense of longing and sadness in any moments of celebration and joy. I suppose the longing to share happy moments with loved ones so far away was always at the back of their minds and as a child I could sense their sadness.

Nowadays, when I make pebre I find myself smiling at the fact that what was once a smell I couldn't stand, is now a smell I very much enjoy — chopped fresh coriander. Its freshness fills me with hope. Pebre is associated with celebrations and fiesta time. It always features at Independence Day festivities in Chile and at barbeque get-togethers with friends and family. It's funny but my children now love pebre and for them it has the same association with good times. My eldest loves it with fresh bread.

Although I married an Englishman and my children are English, I too want them to remember they are half Chilean and feel proud to be Chilean. And with this, comes all the traditions of Chilean food as well as speaking Spanish, but also to remember with respect what their

CHILEAN PEBRE
(CHILE'S VERSION OF SALSA)

grandparents and mum had to go through outside Chile, whilst so many others were not lucky enough to survive a Chilean dictatorship.

Whilst life has a funny way of deciding one's fate, Pebre can help both through the good times and the bad.

Ingredients

5–6 TOMATOES (very ripe if possible).

½ an ONION.

1 WHOLE GREEN CHILLI.

LARGE BUNCH of FRESH CORIANDER.

½ a GREEN PEPPER.

2 CLOVES of FRESH GARLIC.

JUICE of a WHOLE LEMON.

1 tbsp WHITE VINEGAR.

1 tbsp OLIVE OIL.

LARGE PINCH of SALT.

Method

Chop the tomatoes into small cubes and place into a bowl. Then chop the onion and green pepper into small pieces and add to the tomatoes. Crush or chop garlic and add that too.

Now for my favourite part. Hold the bunch of fresh coriander tightly and chop it through. Once all the coriander is chopped in this way, gently hold the end of the knife down onto the chopping board and move the knife back and forth to continue making the pieces of coriander finer before adding them to the bowl.

Cut the chilli in half and de-seed. Then cut it carefully into strips before chopping it into small cubes. Add the chilli to the bowl along with all the remaining ingredients. Mix together and taste to make sure enough salt has been added.

This salsa is traditionally eaten with empanadas, but can accompany many foods and is especially good with barbeques. It also tastes great from one day to the next as the flavours are slowly concentrated.

DR. ROSEMARY LEONARD, MBE
GP and Journalist

From the moment my sons were old enough to swim well, I've taken them away for a week's sailing in the summer and, as they hit their teenage years, having friends along too makes it more fun for them. We like to go to Greece or Turkey, and meals in the evening are usually in a local taverna by a small bay.

One evening in Greece, the weather suddenly changed, the wind came up and it was clear we weren't going to get to a bay with a taverna. Instead, we took shelter in the nearest cove and I was faced with feeding six very hungry lads from the very basic store cupboard ingredients in the galley. This was how Sailing Tomato Rice was born.

Ever since then, my sons insist we have it for dinner one evening when we're on holiday. I haven't called it a risotto because I've only had long grain rice on a boat. On the first occasion we dished it up straight from the saucepan with just a large pile of grated cheese. Now, with more careful menu planning, we serve it with some green salad and, if there are keen carnivores on board, some local sausages.

SAILING TOMATO RICE

ALL QUANTITIES ARE APPROXIMATE. ON A BOAT THERE AREN'T ANY SCALES – YOU JUST CHUCK STUFF INTO A PAN.

Ingredients

1 LARGE (or 2 medium) ONIONS. Add more if you like them.

2 CLOVES OF GARLIC.

1 LARGE TIN (or 2 standard tins) of CHOPPED TOMATOES.

A REALLY GOOD-SIZED DOLLOP of TOMATO KETCHUP (at least a tablespoon).

500g LONG GRAIN RICE.

MEDITERRANEAN HERBS (fresh are better than dried) – MARJORAM, BASIL, OREGANO.

SALT AND PEPPER.

OLIVE OIL for frying.

Method

First fry the onion gently in a small amount of olive oil until soft. Then add the crushed garlic and fry for a few minutes. Add a little more oil, followed by the rice.

Mix with the onions and garlic and fry for a little longer till the rice looks transparent. Then add the rest of the ingredients. The tomato ketchup is really important — it adds much needed sweetness and extra flavour.

Turn the heat down and, stirring occasionally, cook until the water from the tomatoes has been absorbed and the rice is cooked. It usually takes about 20 minutes. If it starts going dry and the rice is still a bit hard, add water as required.

DR. RANJ SINGH
NHS Doctor and TV Presenter

This is my mum's recipe for one of my favourite childhood dishes. Masoor dhal is one of those things that fixes everything, and I can always remember having it when feeling poorly. It's basically a staple in any Indian household! You can dress it up and have it as part of a celebratory banquet, or you can simply have it by itself as a comforting soup. It's the dhal that goes with everything: chapatti, crusty bread, rice or even chips — although don't tell anyone I said that! It's so easy to make that even a non-cook like myself can do it! It's simple, yet somehow perfect,

SERVES 4

Ingredients

TARKA (MASALA MIX):

3 tbsp of COOKING OIL.

1 large chopped ONION.

4 chopped GARLIC CLOVES.

1 tsp of CUMIN SEEDS.

1 or 2 chopped GREEN CHILLIES (depending on how hot you like it!).

1 inch of GINGER (finely chopped).

1 chopped TOMATO.

MY MUM'S MASOOR DHAL

DHAL:

1 cup of SPLIT RED LENTILS (ideally from an Indian store as they cook better).

3 cups of WATER.

1 tsp of TURMERIC.

1 tsp of SALT.

CORIANDER to GARNISH.

Method

Cook the dhal first. Wash and drain the lentils several times to get rid of any grit. Add the water, lentils, salt and turmeric to a large pot and bring it all to simmer. Partly cover the pot and continue to cook on low to medium heat for around 30 minutes (or until the lentils are soft and mushy). You can add more water to get the desired consistency if required.

Then prepare the tarka. Heat the oil in a separate pan and add the onion, garlic and cumin. Cook until light brown. Add the chillies and ginger and cook for a further 2 minutes. Add the tomato and cook for another 2 minutes, stirring regularly.

Add the tarka mix to the dhal and stir in. Garnish with the coriander and voila! So easy! So tasty!

TOM WATT
Actor & Writer

I've been lucky: work has taken me all over the world. And my best memories of countries I've been to are, as often as not, bound up with food I've eaten and the people I ate it with. That said, I'm no expert: I like my food simple, for the most part, and eat it when I'm hungry rather than when I've nothing better to do. I've not eaten meat for the best part of forty years and, maybe because of that, I'm a big fan of the bean in all its forms.

My best-ever, without question, were eaten during the course of one of my best ever jobs: stage-managing a tour of India for GRAEAE, the groundbreaking company of actors with disabilities, back in the mid-1980s. We tipped up in New Delhi and, that same evening, we headed out to explore. I've no idea where we were and I certainly couldn't find my way back there now. But I do remember buying dry chana masala from a street vendor: a funnel of burnt-red little curry-bombs, wrapped in newspaper, and served with a quarter of a lime to set off the spices and a stick of cucumber to balance the sourness of that and the curry itself.

I've ordered chana masala in every curry house I've ever visited since, the quality of the cooking, as far as I'm concerned, is defined by how well the chana brings back memories of late evening sunshine in India and a dusty, crowded Delhi street suddenly brought to a halt by a paper cone full of chickpeas.

DRY KALA CHANA MASALA

4 PORTIONS

Ingredients

1 CUP of BOILED CHANA.

2 tsp CUMIN SEEDS.

1 inch of FRESH GINGER, grated into strips.

2 tsp grated FRESH GARLIC.

2 tsp RED CHILI POWDER.

2 tbsp CORIANDER POWDER.

1 tsp TURMERIC POWDER.

2 tsp GARAM MASALA.

1 or 2 FRESH GREEN CHILIS, chopped.

1 cup CORIANDER LEAVES, chopped.

JUICE of ONE LEMON.

A LITTLE SALT (bear in mind the chana is boiled in salt water).

Method

Wash and soak the chana overnight and then boil (or pressure cook) in salted water until soft.

Heat the oil in a non-stick pan and add the cumin seeds and cook until they start crackling. Add ginger and garlic and cook until they soften.

Drain off most of the cooking water from the boiled chana and then add the chana to the pan. Stir and cook for a couple of minutes.

Stir in all the other spices: red chili powder, coriander powder, turmeric powder, garam masala and a little salt. Mix together and cook for five minutes or so. Add a little water if it starts sticking.

Throw in the chopped green chilis and cook for another couple of minutes. Just before serving, add chopped coriander leaves and lemon juice. Stir them in but do not overcook. Serve dry chana masala with Indian bread, or on its own with lemon or lime wedges and a stick of cucumber.

JIM CORR
Irish Musician and member of *The Corrs*

No animals die in the making of this dish!
I've been vegetarian for about three years and that transition has been one of the best decisions I've made, not just for the animals but for health as well. We do not need to eat meat to survive, in fact we thrive without it. So I was searching for a healthy vegetable chilli recipe that was relatively quick to make, full of flavour and pleasing to the conscience.

This is a variation of a recipe given to me by a friend. I've always loved chilli, it's comfort food, and it's easy to increase the amount of ingredients to satisfy a larger group of people. It's such a fun dish to make and to eat with friends. Living close to an organic farm allows me to easily source the best of healthy ingredients without worrying about nasty pesticides and chemicals. Once preparation is done it only takes about 30 minutes to cook.

Ingredients
ALL ORGANIC IF YOU KNOW WHAT'S GOOD FOR YOU :-)

1 ONION diced.

Handful of MUSHROOMS diced.

1½ CARROTS diced.

1 CELERY STICK diced.

VEGETARIAN CHILLI

1 RED PEPPER diced.

3 CLOVES GARLIC chopped finely or through a garlic press.

Handful FRESH CORIANDER chopped.

SEA SALT / PINK HIMALAYAN to taste (I find about 1 tsp works but taste periodically to check)

BLACK PEPPER milled.

½–1 tsp GROUND CHILLI POWDER (according to taste and whether you use the large red chilli pepper below).

1 LARGE RED CHILLI PEPPER chopped finely (or add more chilli powder).

1 tsp GROUND CUMIN.

1 tsp GROUND CORIANDER.

½ tsp SMOKED PAPRIKA.

1½ tsp GROUND VEGETABLE STOCK.

1 tin chopped TOMATOES.

1 tin RED KIDNEY BEANS drained and washed.

¼ cup PURE WATER.

JUICE of 1 LIME.

Method

Fry the onion for a couple of minutes in some light olive oil or coconut oil at medium temperature.

Add the mushrooms, carrots and celery and fry for 10 minutes on a low heat. Add the garlic, red pepper, kidney beans and all the spices. Give it a stir and let it cook for 1 minute. Add the tinned tomatoes, the vegetable stock and a ¼ cup of pure water (pour it into the left over tin of tomato juice and shake before adding).

Now add the sea salt and pepper, freshly squeezed lime juice, and the fresh coriander. Leave to simmer gently for 20–25 mins, checking the seasoning halfway through.

Serve on top of wholegrain brown basmati rice for great flavour and nutrition (vegan). You can also serve with sour cream, yogurt or baked milk kefir (vegetarian). Garnish with fresh coriander.

MY MUM'S SMOKED MACKEREL PÂTÉ

Ingredients

2 WHOLE SMOKED MACKEREL.

1 tsp GRATED HORSERADISH.

2 tsp DIJON MUSTARD.

2 tbsp CRÈME FRAÎCHE.

JUICE of HALF a LEMON.

100g UNSALTED BUTTER.

GROUND BLACK PEPPER.

Method

Remove the skin from the smoked mackerel and place in the blender. Add the other ingredients and blend into a paste. So simple and utterly delicious!

DR DAWN HARPER
GP and TV Presenter

As children we used to holiday in the small town of Newport on the Pembrokeshire coast each year. I have very fond memories of messing around with boats all day and fishing for mackerel with hand lines.

When we caught them we would bring them home for Dad to smoke in the garden on his small tin smoker and Mum would make this pâté and serve it with a hot French stick, freshly baked in the local bakery. It is still one of my favourite starters. This year I bought my other half, who is an excellent chef, a Magimix for Christmas and it was the first thing he made with it!

I have had so many patients who have found our local Maggie's a real support through their cancer journey. It is a absolute pleasure to support the charity. Long may they continue their invaluable work.

Ingredients

PIE CRUST:

220g PLAIN FLOUR.

100g BUTTER.

PINCH of BLACK PEPPERCORNS.

LOBSTER MAC 'N' CHEESE:

1 LOBSTER, ROUGHLY 350–500g (FROZEN, FRESH OR TAILS – WHATEVER YOU CAN GET).

1 ONION.

3 CLOVES OF GARLIC.

50g UNSALTED BUTTER.

1 tbsp PLAIN FLOUR.

1 tsp ENGLISH MUSTARD.

1 tsp FENNEL SEEDS.

1 tbsp SMOKED PAPRIKA.

1 litre WHOLE MILK.

300g OF PASTA (BECAUSE THESE PIES ARE SMALL, A SOUP PASTA LIKE MARGHERITINE OR MACARONI WORKS BEST).

180g OF MATURE CHEDDAR (PREFERABLY SCOTTISH AND THEREFORE ORANGE OR MIX HALF RED LEICESTER AND HALF CHEDDAR).

1 PACKET OF SCOTTISH OATCAKES.

JAMES BRANDON
Masterchef 2017 Contestant and Food Blogger

As a child of the armed forces I had the privilege of living abroad for many years. I experienced both life in both Canada and Germany and was exposed to some great food. But my favourite food memory always reminds me of Scotland.

Every year we would make the trip to visit 'Granny Motherwell' often driving a total of 15 hours. The journeys were sound tracked by Aqua's *Barbie Girl*, the Spice Girls and the Proclaimers.

No trip to Motherwell would be complete without a visit to the butchers for a Macaroni Pie. Cheese, elbow pasta and scotch pastry are a combination that is pure comfort. I have never been able to hold back and have always blistered my upper mouth from the molten orange cheese that sits on top.

One of the main reasons I remember these pies so fondly is they were usually the supper we had after leaving my gran, and driven hours and hours back to our home. Eating these macaroni pies straight from the oven, after sitting in the car for so long, somehow made it feel like part of Scotland was with us.

I moved back to Scotland after university and this pie is a take on my experience of the great produce both on land and sea. Sadly, we lost Granny Motherwell to cancer in 2012, and I hope this pie recipe will help to raise the funds to put an end to cancer one day.

LOBSTER MAC 'N' CHEESE PIES

Method

Before you start, you can choose to drop the lobster completely from this recipe. Just make the macaroni cheese, leaving out the steps that include the lobster. Preheat the oven to 180°C, gas mark 4. Place the pie crust ingredients into a food processor and pulse until they resemble fine breadcrumbs. Add a tablespoon of water at a time until the mix starts to come together in a dough. (You can do this by hand if you don't have a processor.) Form the dough into a tight ball, wrap it in cling film and let it rest for 20 minutes.

Next, you need to cook the lobster (if frozen see the pack for details). In a pan, bring salty water to the boil. Submerge the lobster and cover with a lid for five to eight minutes depending on the size of your lobster. Remove and let it cool down. Then crack open the lobster pulling out all of the meat. Be careful to avoid the stomach sack that is behind the head.

In salted boiling water cook your pasta, al dente if possible as when the pies are in the oven it will continue to take on the liquid. Finely dice the onions and garlic and put in a pan on a low heat with the fennel seeds. After 10 minutes add the butter. Once melted, stir in the flour to form a roux. Cook off the flour for two to three minutes and then add the milk one cup at time, whisking as you go until you have a thick sauce. Throw pasta into the sauce and mix it well. Then set it aside till it comes to room temperature.

For my pies I use poaching rings to form them. Grease the rings with butter and lay them down on greaseproof paper. Roll out the pastry on a lightly floured surface. The same thickness as a pound coin ideally.

Using greaseproof paper and baking beans or rice fill the pies ready for blind baking. Bake in the oven for around 15 minutes. If small cracks develop you can brush with an egg wash to form a barrier.

At this point take your oatcakes, roughly chop them up and add lots of pepper. Remove your pie cases from the oven, fill each one with your macaroni mixture and then top with the oatcake crumble. These now go back into the oven for 40 minutes at 180°C to finish.

SHARRON DAVIES, MBE
OLYMPIC SWIMMER

No real story, just a tasty recipe the whole family likes. It's easy and can be adapted to everyone's taste.

You can add all sorts of vegetables like sweet corn, broccoli or peas, a great way of getting kids to eat them rather hidden!

Adding parsley to the sauce is also nice. That's the beauty of this recipe — add or take away what you like, substitute salmon for white fish, or even have both. It's easy to adapt.

And if you want to make it slightly more fancy, at a supper party with friends for instance, slice a large tomato and place on top before adding the rest of the grated cheese. Then serve with a large crispy salad.

I'm a super cook really!

FISH PIE

Ingredients

500g of POTATOES.

1 SPOON of BUTTER.

250g of MILK.

2 FILLETS of FRESH SALMON.

100g of FRESH PRAWNS.

100g of SCALLOPS.

PINCH of SALT and PEPPER.

100g of GRATED CHEESE.

Method

Pre-heat your oven to 180°C.

Peel and boil the potatoes until soft and then mash, adding a little butter and milk.

Put the remaining butter and milk into a pan and heat.

Add all fish to the remaining milk and butter and gently poach — breaking into small pieces (this should take roughly 5 minutes) then add the seasoning, and 3/4 of the cheese.

Put the fish that is in a sauce into an oven-proof dish and then layer on the mash potato.

Finally, sprinkle on the remaining cheese and put into the oven for 15 minutes or until the top starts to turn a golden brown.

TO MAKE 2-4 SANDWICHES –
DEPENDING ON HOW HUNGRY YOU FEEL!

Ingredients

BREAD – NICE FRESH WHITE /
BROWN / SOURDOUGH OF YOUR CHOICE.

A HANDFUL of CAPERS.

A HANDFUL of CORNICHONS.

ZEST OF 1 LEMON.

FOR THE TARTAR SAUCE:

3 BANANA SHALLOTS.

1 SMALL BUNCH of DILL.

1 SMALL BUNCH of FLAT LEAF PARSLEY.

10ml WHITE WINE VINEGAR.

200ml OF MAYONNAISE
(good shop bought would be fine).

1 tbsp of DIJON MUSTARD.

FOR THE FISH FINGERS:

300g sustainable WHITE FISH
(COD, HADDOCK, COLEY, LING).

BREADCRUMBS – either PANKO or any STALE
/ OLDER BREAD dried out and blitzed into crumbs.

200ml MILK.

5 EGGS.

150g PLAIN FLOUR.

FISH FINGER SANDWICH

We serve them in wonderful freshly baked bread. My personal favourite is with malted brown but it tastes great with any of our breads. And to top it all, our own homemade tartar sauce. I have grown up a little though in the past 48 years — I quite like it with an accompanying salad — something like tomato and rocket with a balsamic and oil dressing. Now, if there was just a way to form all that into a hedgehog?

DAVID ORME
Owner of The Find,
Cheltenham

It all started in 1970 in Solihull. Aged 5 and recently started at school, I used to go home every Wednesday with my best friend, Richard Morris (who I haven't seen in 45 years now). It was one week at my house, another week at his, but otherwise the same routine: lunch in front of the TV (Mr Benn, and Mungo, Mary and Midge I seem to recall), and fish fingers. Always fish fingers.

In those days it was typically a fish finger hedgehog — a pile of mashed potatoes with fish fingers stuck in to create a hedgehog. It didn't come that way but that's how it always ended up. I still do that even now at home, and my daughters stare at me with that "how old are you?" look.

Fish fingers are so easy to cook that if I get in late, I often think that's what I'll have — even when there are other delicacies in the fridge. It's my ultimate comfort food. The food that makes me feel happy and floods me with happy memories.

Consequently, when I started The Find, there was never any question that there would be a fish finger sandwich on the menu. Obviously we couldn't use Birds Eye (although I confess to still eating those at home sometimes), so we created our own fish fingers, made from fresh fish delivered daily and homemade breadcrumbs.

Method

First, the tartar sauce. Using a stick blender or a food processor, blend all the ingredients bar the capers and the cornichons. Once everything is mixed in, dice the capers and the cornichons to the size you prefer (chunky or not) and fold through. You can do all this without a processor but you'll have to dice by hand. Lastly, cover and refrigerate.

Now for the fish. First, cut it into chunky finger-style pieces ready to be breadcrumbed. Then prepare your 'pane station'. Set up a line of three tubs containing flour, whisked eggs and milk, and breadcrumbs, respectively. Pane your fish pieces by dipping them along the station in the same order, ensuring they are well covered. You can also give them an extra coat by repeating the process using the egg mix and breadcrumbs.

Have a fryer with clean oil in and set it to 180°C. Once at the right temperature, carefully lower your fish fingers into the fryer until golden brown. After 4—5 minutes, cut one in half to ensure they're cooked through.

Grab your chosen bread. Put the tartar sauce and some salad on the bottom piece of bread followed by your fish fingers. Place down the top piece of bread and there you have it — a great fish finger sandwich!

RYAN RILEY
Food Writer and Stylist.
Founder of Life Kitchen.

I lost my mum to cancer when I was 18. Inspired by her, I wanted to use my career as a food writer and stylist to help people going through the same experience, and so I launched Life Kitchen.

Life Kitchen offers free cookery courses to people with cancer. They work on building flavours and stimulating the senses as people often lose their ability to taste or find their tastes change dramatically while going through chemotherapy.

There's a range of dishes I teach people to make on the courses and harissa salmon and harissa cauliflower are two of my favourites. I thought it would be great to share them and by doing so get involved with helping Maggie's.

I hope you enjoy these complementary dishes as much as I do!

HARISSA SALMON WITH FENNEL YOGHURT SALAD

Ingredients

FOR THE SALMON:

2 WILD SALMON FILLETS.

2 tbsp HARISSA PASTE.

1 tbsp OLIVE OIL.

1 FENNEL BULB, cut into matchsticks.

3 tbsp YOGHURT.

1 LIME, juice and zest.

1 tsp NIGELLA SEEDS.

1 LEMON.

FOR THE CAULIFLOWER:

CAULIFLOWER LEAVES.

2 tbsp HARISSA PASTE.

1 tbsp OLIVE OIL.

SEA SALT.

Method

Mix together the harissa and oil and coat the salmon fillets generously.

Place into a 180°C oven for 8 minutes. Remove from the oven and set aside.

Cut the fennel into thin matchsticks. Add to a bowl with the yoghurt, lime zest and lime juice, and toss together.

Sprinkle over the nigella seeds and serve with a wedge of lemon. Season to taste.

For the cauliflower. Mix together the harissa, oil and salt and brush over the cauliflower leaves. Roast at 180°C for 20 minutes until the outer leaves are crispy and delicious!

PIMPED UP MACKEREL AND RICE

Dad died on the 1st August that year and I will forever be grateful that I was able to have the luxury of spending that time with him and giving something back. In his memory, I founded Eat Life, a nutritional brand offering high-calorie, high-protein foods and drinks in convenient, small portions with the aim of helping anyone out there who is facing the same struggle to take on enough calories and nutrients. And I always think of him when I eat mackerel.

SAMANTHA WILLIAMSON
Founder of Eat Life.
Winner of our Website Competition.

The first nine months of 2015 was maybe the most difficult, emotional and yet rewarding time of my life. My Dad had been diagnosed with terminal acute myeloid leukaemia and I moved in to help take care of him, not really believing that the worst would happen. There was a lot of medical stuff to deal with but we also laughed a lot, put together family-tree photo albums and spent a guilty amount of time watching daytime TV. Judge Rinder was a yes, property makeover programs an absolute no (much to my distress).

As the illness and chemo took hold, Dad lost weight, his appetite and his energy levels. I earned myself the nickname 'Naggy Daughter' for continuously trying get him to eat and hiding extra calories in his meals — or 'pimping them up' as he would call it. His one go-to meal, when nothing else worked, was mackerel and rice. Sounded horrible to me, but I made it and he swore it was delicious. Apparently the strong flavour of the mackerel ticked his tastebuds and woke them up.

Not wanting to disappoint his expectations, I even managed to pimp that up with horseradish mayo mixed into the mackerel and olive oil stirred through the rice And then I tasted it, and you know what, he was right! I prefer it with smoked mackerel fillet from the supermarket but he was equally happy with a tin.

Ingredients

100g SMOKED MACKEREL FILLET (that's a bit less than half a pack in the main supermarkets and use the plain ones not peppered as the pepper gets stuck in teeth or can be a bit sore for a sensitive mouth). Alternatively use a tin of mackerel fillets, preferably in oil (approx. 300 kcals).

1 tbsp of MAYONNAISE (approx. 95 kcals).

1 flat tsp of HORSERADISH SAUCE (approx. 15 kcals).

½ A PACK (125g) OF MICROWAVEABLE WHITE RICE (approx. 200 kcals).

1 tbsp of OLIVE OIL (approx. 120 kcals)

Total calories in dish approx. 730 kcals.

Method

In a bowl mix the mayonnaise and horseradish together.

Chop or mash up the mackerel and stir into the horseradish mayonnaise. Mix and season to taste.

Heat the rice in the microwave then stir the olive oil through it until throughly mixed.

Serve the mackerel mix on the rice and let the tastebuds be tickled.

If you want it to look pretty, you can pop a cherry tomato on the top but you'll be fighting a bit of a losing battle...

Ingredients

FOR THE CHORIZO:

2 tbsp OLIVE OIL.

1 RED ONION, roughly chopped.

1 GARLIC CLOVE, roughly chopped.

100g / 3½oz CHORIZO, cut into chunks.

2–3 SPRIGS THYME

50g / 1¾oz BLACK OLIVES, stones removed

8 CHERRY TOMATOES.

SALT and FRESHLY GROUND BLACK PEPPER.

FOR THE SEA BASS:

1 LARGE SEA BASS, head removed, scaled and gutted (your fishmonger or supermarket can do this, don't panic).

SMALL BUNCH FRESH THYME.

MAURICE GRAN
Scriptwriter and Keen Amateur Brain Surgeon.

It was the summer of 1979; my writing partner Laurence and I sat in the director's box at a London TV studio, watching the dress rehearsal of *Holding The Fort*, the very first episode of our very first sitcom. Everyone was anxious, because the ITV unions had been threatening a pay strike for weeks. Inevitably, halfway through the rehearsal, a determined and intimidating union official barrelled into the box and ordered the director to stop directing.

The strike seemed to last forever (it was almost Christmas by the time the management caved in), so to cheer myself up I blew my entire writer's fee on a three week trip around the promised land of California. I still remember the infinite beaches, the huge burgers, and the monstrous air-conditioned Chevrolet I hired. The pound was worth two dollars back then — God knows why, Britain was nearly bankrupt — which brings me to the Patagonian Tooth Fish. Of course nobody calls it Patagonian Tooth Fish. In the ritzy San Diego seafood restaurant it was billed simply as grilled sea bass. My wife and I had barely heard of sea bass in those innocent days, but whatever its name, it was the best, juiciest, tastiest hunk of barbecued flesh I have ever eaten.

The following year we eventually made the first season of *Holding the Fort*, and it was a mid-sized hit, so Laurence and I were commissioned to write the second series pretty damn quickly. Patricia Hodge, one of our stars, kindly

PATAGONIAN TOOTH FISH

said we could use her villa in Spain as a writers' retreat. We wrote two episodes in two weeks. When we weren't retreating we looked for interesting places to eat, which is how we found ourselves in a smart restaurant in Valencia, which offered, as the especial del dia, sea bass. Of course we ordered it. When it arrived, instead of the massive juicy fish steak I'd told Laurence to expect, we were each given a measly bony little fish, its dead mouth pouting through a scanty salad.

I tried to complain, but the manager spoke no English and we spoke less Spanish. A helpful British expat tried to interpret. "This gentleman says he has eaten sea bass and this isn't sea bass," he explained in Spanish.

The manager was outraged. He screamed at the hapless Brit, as if he was the one complaining, and completely ignored us. We did the only thing two English gentlemen could under the circumstances. Slowly and quietly we sneaked out of the restaurant and left them to their shouting.

Decades later sea bass has become one of the staples of our national fishy diet. As Patagonian Tooth Fish is now a rare and protected species, here is one of my favourite recipes for the smaller, but equally tasty European version. (It's from the BBC's website, but what the hell, I pay my license fee!)

ROASTED SEA BASS WITH CHORIZO, RED ONION AND CHERRY TOMATOES

Method

Preheat the oven to 190°C, 375°F, gas mark 5. Heat the olive oil in a frying pan over a medium heat. Add the onion, garlic and chorizo. Fry for 4–5 minutes until the oil runs out of the chorizo and the onions soften.

Add the thyme, olives and tomatoes and stir to combine. Season well with salt and freshly ground black pepper, before transferring the mixture to an ovenproof dish.

Using a sharp knife, slash skin of the sea bass diagonally along each side so that the flesh is exposed and place sprigs of thyme into the slashes. Season the sea bass with salt and freshly ground black pepper and place on top of the chorizo mixture. Drizzle over the olive oil and cook in the oven for 20–25 minutes, until the fish is tender and cooked all the way through. Serve with something green and something starchy. Chips and peas works. So do roast new potatoes and a mixed leaf salad.

25

KIM BAILEY
Race Horse Trainer

It might sound strange to anybody outside racing but the Cheltenham Festival week is possibly the busiest week of my year. It all starts several days before the meeting itself with many late nights doing Cheltenham preview evenings for selection and thoughts, followed by the usual early starts (5.30am). So by the time the first day's racing arrives, it's been full on entertaining. And now we're saddling runners and, we hope, winners, at the meeting, which is of course why I do it and why we all go — to see National Hunt Racing at its very best.

Mrs Bailey (or rightly, Clare) knows that time is short and we need to be able to eat on the go at any time of the day, and that usually means very early in the morning, so she cooks a huge pot of Kedgeree which will last the week. Yes you can reheat it several times without ruining the taste. Hard to believe but, as I love Kedgeree, I will forgive any overdcooked egg. (Anyway, you can always add one or two fresh eggs later.)

It's a hugely popular dish which is always welcomed by guests staying and owners visiting. So much so that many years ago one of my owners was so amazed that he said "I have not come all this way (from Essex) to have a bloody risotto." He must have been expecting the full English. Now follows Mrs B's recipe...

RACING KEDGEREE

Ingredients

2 EGGS, boiled for 8 minutes (this gives a lovely creamy yolk, if you prefer hard boiled cook for longer).

680g undyed SMOKED HADDOCK FILLETS, boned.

2 BAY LEAVES.

170g LONG-GRAIN OR BASMATI RICE.

SALT and GROUND BLACK PEPPER.

1 MEDIUM ONION, finely chopped.

1 CLOVE of GARLIC, finely chopped.

3 tbsp PATAKS BALTI CURRY PASTE, or equivalent. (If no paste to hand use 2 tsp of curry powder.)

2 LEMONS.

2 good handfuls of CHOPPED CORIANDER.

Method

Put the haddock in a frying pan with the bay leaves and bring to a simmer for five minutes till cooked. Drain, let it cool a little, then remove skin and flake the fish. Set aside.

Cook the rice in salted water for 10 minutes then drain and rinse with cold water. (This can be done in advance and kept in the fridge.)

Melt the butter in a pan, add the onion and garlic and cook for five minutes until soft.

Add the curry paste or powder (to your taste) and cook for a couple more minutes.

Add the juice of one lemon. Shell and cut the boiled eggs into quarters.

Add the fish and rice into the onion pan and stir gently to warm through. Then stir in the eggs and coriander.

Serve warm with wedges of the second lemon.

P J CROOK, MBE
Artist

One of the most memorable meals that I have enjoyed was when Richard and I were in Sète in the South of France where I had been invited to hold the inaugural exhibition at the magnificently extended Musée Paul Valéry, overlooking the Mediterranean.

During the hanging of the exhibition, with the sun flooding through the tall narrow windows, we marvelled at the relaxed way the exhibition staff did everything, stopping at lunchtime for a two hour break and wishing each other bon appetit, and how this contrasted with the fast moving pace of the galleries in Paris and London, where a sandwich lunch was grabbed between tasks.

We were joined at the grand opening by my Paris dealers, Alain and Michelle Blondel, and were all invited to dinner by the director, André Fraises, who took us to the enchanting restaurant that he owned and ran with his sons.

Outside, we were fascinated to see oyster beds, so it was no surprise to find enormous platters piled high with the most exquisite cooked oysters filling our table.

They were so plentiful and so delicious that we filled ourselves with this wonderful oyster feast only to discover when they removed the empty platters that they were replaced with the main course — plates full of superbly cooked monkfish.

Now, when we're cooking special dinners and there's an R in the month, Richard often prepares these.

OYSTERS FROM SÈTE

Ingredients and Method

Allow at least half a dozen oysters per person — the more the better.

Schuck the oysters, that is remove the flat half of the shell and loosen the fish, whilst retaining as much liquid as possible.

Place them all on a baking tray so that they support each other.

Add two or three thin slivers of garlic, a sprig of parsley, topped with a thin slice of Gruyère cheese.

You don't need to add salt as oysters have their own fresh from the sea.

Place in a hot oven for about 15 minutes until the cheese is bubbling and golden.

DINAH JEFFERIES
Author

Nasi Goreng is the Indonesian name for fried rice and variations of a similar recipe exist across South-East Asia where many of my books are set. It originated as a breakfast dish to use up the leftover rice, meat fish and vegetables, supplementing them with eggs and fresh ingredients like lettuce, cucumber, spring onions or tomatoes. This is my husband's version of the recipe, based on the dish I knew from my childhood spent in Malaysia.

Ingredients

4 CUPS COOKED WHITE LONG GRAIN RICE, such as BASMATI.
175g COOKED CHICKEN MEAT.
(boneless, skinless, shredded into pieces).
175g COOKED PRAWNS (without shells).
100g LONG GREEN BEANS. (French type or similar) chopped into 1.5 to 2.0 cm long pieces.
60g FINELY CHOPPED SHALLOTS.
1 MEDIUM CARROT, finely diced.
150g SPINACH, lightly chopped.

FOR SAMBAL TUMIS: (a mixture of spice pastes):
1½ tbsp SHRIMP PASTE (Malay Belacan is best but the Thai version is widely available and works almost as well).
1 tbsp CHILLI PASTE (try different varieties. and adjust quantity to your taste).
½ tbsp DARK MISO PASTE.
½ tbsp TOMATO PUREE.
½ tbsp GARLIC AND GINGER PASTE. (jars of ready prepared paste are widely available).

FOR STIR FRYING:
2 or 3 tbsp RAPESEED OIL or COCONUT OIL.
2 tbsp LIME JUICE.
2 tbsp KICAP MANIS (a Malaysian sweet soya sauce now available from most major supermarkets).
1 tbsp LIGHT SOYA SAUCE.
8 SPRING ONIONS, trimmed and finely chopped.
Salt and pepper to taste.

FOR GARNISHES:
175g FINELY SLICED RED ONIONS.
500ml COLD WATER with about 2 tbsp of SALT stirred in.
4 EGGS.
ABOUT ¼ CUP OF VEGETABLE OIL.

PLUS, ANY TWO OF THE BELOW or more if you adjust the quantity to suit:
100g OF SHREDDED CRISP LETTUCE, SUCH A LITTLE GEM, sliced into strips about 5mm wide.
3 SLICED MEDIUM SIZED FRESH TOMATOES (get the sweetest you can).
½ CUCUMBER, sliced into small batons.

MALAY NASI GORENG

Method

Prepare the crispy fried onions. Put the finely sliced red onions for the garnish into the salted cold water for about one minute, drain well and pat dry with a kitchen towel. Heat ¼ cup of vegetable oil in a small saucepan, putting just one or two slices of the finely sliced red onions in. When they float to the top and gently sizzle then add all the rest and fry until a dark golden colour, stirring every so often. Don't let them burn. When done, use a slotted spoon and place the onions on some kitchen towels to absorb any extra oil. You can keep them warm in a low oven.

Prepare the green beans. Boil some water, drop in the sliced green beans and simmer for no more than two minutes. Drain and put to one side.

If the rice has been kept in fridge overnight, then allow it to reach room temperature. Fluff it up with a fork, just before starting to cook all the other ingredients.

Prepare the paste. In a small bowl, add all the Sambal Tumis ingredients and stir until they are all blended together. Heat two or three tablespoons of oil in a wok until hot and fry the chopped shallots until they just start to caramelise and are tender and translucent. Add the Sambal paste and cook it until the oil separates from the paste. Turn down the heat and keep stirring for a further two minutes.

Add the diced carrots and the green beans followed by the chicken, lime juice, and kicap manis. Stir well to blend and coat with the spicy mixture. Then add the cooked rice followed by the cooked prawns. Stir all together well for three or four minutes, then add the washed shredded spinach and half the spring onion, stirring well into the rice and letting the spinach wilt for a few minutes. Add the soya sauce and season with salt and pepper to taste. Remove the wok from the heat and set aside.

Lastly, cook the eggs, frying them till the edges are crispy but the yolks still runny or, better still, made into thin omelettes which are rolled and sliced into 5mm wide strips to create a sort of whole egg noodle.

Serve onto warmed plates with a helping of the rice mixture, topped with some egg, the remaining spring onions and the crispy onions. Add some cucumber, lettuce and sliced tomato as you wish.

GINNY ELLIOT, MBE

I was brought up in the Far East and spent many happy days riding ponies, swimming and running around with no shoes on, being a tearaway and a general nuisance.

My food memory is Nasi Goreng. This was my absolute favourite and was used on many occasions in negotiations between my Mother and myself: good behaviour — Nasi Goreng; bad behaviour — none for days, if not weeks!

I have made this dish ever since I was finally allowed the secret recipe. It takes me back to those wonderful days every time I eat it.

SERVES 4

Ingredients
FOR THE PASTE:

3 tbs GROUNDNUT OIL.

4 cloves GARLIC.

2 SHALLOTS chopped.

½ oz PEANUTS.

GOOD BEHAVIOUR NASI GORENG

6 medium RED CHILLIES chopped.

1 tbs TOMATO PURÉE.

½ tsp DRIED SHRIMP PASTE.

1 tbs SWEET SOY SAUCE.

8oz LONG GRAIN RICE.

2 LARGE EGGS.

SUNFLOWER OIL for frying.

6 SHALLOTS.

8oz best quality COOKED PRAWNS.

6oz MACKEREL.

½ tbsp SOY SAUCE.

¼ of a CUCUMBER
peeled and sliced into 2 inch strips.

4 SPRING ONIONS

Method

Put all the paste ingredients in a blender for 2 minutes.

Cook the rice for 9 minutes from boiling and drain well.

Lightly oil the mackerel and grill for 4 minutes each side.

Use the eggs to make an omelette and set aside.

Fry the shallots until crispy.

Heat a wok with remaining oil from the fried shallots. Add the paste, then add the rice over about 2 minutes, stirring constantly to avoid burning. Add the prawns, onions, sliced omelette and flaked mackerel. Lastly, add the soy sauce and spring onions.

Serve immediately.

JANE DEVONSHIRE
Masterchef 2016 Winner.

Author of *Hassle Free, Gluten Free*.

During treatment for cancer, this is a recipe that when I was ill the children could cook for me and the family. It's one pot using simple ingredients but really packs a taste punch and it's a bit different.

SERVES 4–6.

Ingredients

1 MEDIUM-SIZED CHICKEN, about 1.8kg (4lb).

1 BULB OF GARLIC, halved horizontally.

A LARGE BUNCH of FRESH THYME.

1 LEMON, halved.

OLIVE OIL.

BUTTER.

SALT and PEPPER.

750g (1lb 10oz) NEW POTATOES.

2 RED ONIONS, peeled and cut into chunks.

2 RED PEPPERS, cut in 2.5cm (1in) squares.

1 YELLOW PEPPER, cut in 2.5cm (1in) square.

SIMPLE ONE-POT ROAST CHICKEN

FOR THE SAUCE:

2 heaped tbsp CRÈME FRAÎCHE.

SALT and PEPPER.

JUICE of 1–2 LEMONS.

Method

Preheat the oven to 200°C/fan 180°C/gas 6. Remove the string from the chicken and put half of the garlic into the cavity with half of the thyme and lemon.

Put the chicken in a roasting pan, cover it with some olive oil and dot with butter. Season with salt and pepper and scatter the remaining thyme over. Roast in the oven for 45 minutes.

Meanwhile put the potatoes in a pan of salted water over a high heat and boil until tender. Drain and set aside.

Take the chicken out of the oven, remove it from the pan and set aside on a plate. Put the potatoes, red onion and the remaining lemon and garlic in the roasting pan and toss them in the juices, adding a little olive oil if they seem dry.

Put the chicken on top and return to the oven for 15 minutes, then take it out again and add the peppers. Return to the oven for 30 minutes. When the thighs of the chicken pull away from the body easily and the juices run clear, remove it from the oven, transfer it to a plate and leave to rest for 15 minutes.

Turn up the oven to 220°C/fan 200°C/gas 7 and put the vegetables back inside for 10 minutes until soft. Remove from the oven, lift the vegetables out of the pan and set aside with the chicken.

To make the sauce, use a spoon to remove the excess fat from the juices in the pan, then place the pan on the hob. Heat gently and add the crème fraîche, salt and pepper and lemon juice to taste, then bring to the boil. Remove from the heat and pour into a small bowl.

Return the vegetables to the pan and place the chicken on top, then serve with the sauce alongside.

JAMES SIMPSON DANIEL
Former Gloucester and England International Rugby Player

Being sportsmen meant that we were often encouraged to eat healthily in order to get the necessary fuels required to keep our bodies where they needed to be on a day-to-day basis. Now clearly we didn't always stick to the rules and some of us less than others!

However, what that did mean was eating lots of protein, and some of us less able cooks used to just prepare chicken over and over again. With that in mind we used to look for as many variations of cooking chicken that we could manage, so the dish I'm sharing is a terribly simple recipe but a favourite that I still cook now.

And to answer some of my ex-colleagues comments, no it doesn't involve prawn cocktail crisps or tomato ketchup! I hope you enjoy!

MICHELIN STAR CHICKEN

Ingredients

4 skinless CHICKEN BREASTS.

1 tub of PHILADELPHIA SOFT CHEESE.

1 jar of SUN-DRIED TOMATO PESTO PASTE.

1 RED CHILLI.

1 pack of CHERRY TOMATOES.

BREADCRUMBS (PANKO CRUMBS are fine if you haven't made your own).

OLIVE OIL.

MALDON SEA SALT FLAKES.

BLACK PEPPER.

PAPRIKA.

Method

Mix the Philadelphia in a bowl with the pesto paste until the consistency is smooth.

Roughly chop the chilli and add to the the mix. Season with salt and black pepper.

Place the chicken breasts into a large roasting dish, then spoon the mixture over the top so that all areas are covered.

Next, spoon over the breadcrumbs followed by a dusting of paprika for a lovely scent.

Lightly season with salt flakes.

Place the chicken into the middle of an oven preheated to 180°C and cook for 25 minutes. Don't use a high oven shelf or the breadcrumbs will burn (I learnt that the hard way).

Place the cherry tomatoes in a separate oven tray. Drizzle them with olive oil and season with salt and black pepper. Add this to the oven when the chicken has 15 minutes remaining.

I also do this for vegetarians, using extra veg such as celery and peppers and substituting veg stock for the chicken stock..

LISA DAWSON
Interiors Writer and Blogger.

This is one of my all time favourites. I'd always been a pretty average and very lazy cook in that I was a big one pot meal fan. Anything that restricted the amount of washing up or work I needed to do was always a bonus. This recipe became my dinner party staple — teamed with naan bread and sour cream it was a winner every time. I could prepare it in advance and then chuck it in the oven 40 minutes before everyone arrived, which meant it left loads of time for pre dinner drinks and chat.

Since having children, inviting people over to our house to socialise was definitely the easy option and this was the perfect easy meal. In fact, I don't think I ever served it to anyone who didn't love it!

Five years ago, I was diagnosed with breast cancer and had six rounds of chemotherapy — my taste buds were completely gone and nothing tasted good. I'd make Lebanese Chicken and add loads of extra chilli for punch and extra fennel to bypass my flavour vacuum. It's still my husband Joe's favourite meal and brings back many happy memories.

Okay so here it is. It is a well loved recipe from about 12 years ago!

LEBANESE CHICKEN WITH FENNEL

SERVES 4.

Ingredients

4 CHICKEN BREASTS OR THIGHS, whatever you like best, cut into chunks.

1 FENNEL BULB.

1 RED ONION.

3 PRESERVED LEMONS (in a jar).

200g BULGAR WHEAT.

3 tbsp OF PLAIN FLOUR.

1 tsp CINNAMON. 1 tsp FENNEL SEED. 1 tsp GROUND CUMIN. 1 tsp CHILLI FLAKES or POWDER. 1 tsp SEA SALT. 1 tsp BLACK PEPPER.

BUNCH of ROSEMARY, chopped.

A PINT of CHICKEN STOCK.

A LARGE GLASS of WHITE WINE.

2 NAAN BREAD and SOUR CREAM to serve.

OLIVE OIL for cooking.

Method

Use a heavy casserole dish that can be used on the hob and in the oven. Put all the spices, flour and seasoning into a bowl and coat the chicken. Fry the chicken off so it's browned, and place to the side.

Chop the fennel (removing the tops), red onion and preserved lemon into chunks and cook on a moderate heat, together with the chopped rosemary, until soft. Add the bulgar wheat and excess flour from the bowl and mix in with the veg.

Throw in the wine and cook gently until the liquid is absorbed. Place your chicken on top of the veg and bulgar wheat mixture and then add chicken stock until it covers the grains.

Cover with a lid and cook at 180°C for 45 mins. Garnish with the fennel tops and serve with sour cream and naan bread.

When I began chemotherapy my pals rallied around wanting to do what they could to make things a little easier. One of my besties, Rebecca, lives around the corner from my parents where I'd hole myself up to ride out the worst of the side effects. Without fail every chemo cycle she'd come over armed with a massive batch of her special chicken broth. Full to the brim with ingredients to boost my immune system, this was a life-saver!

During treatment you become mega weak and I barely had the energy to hold a conversation let alone get culinary in the kitchen. Being able to just wallop a bowl of this

hearty treat into the microwave when hunger would strike was a dream and took a lot of drama out of meal times. This meant I was getting my calories in a nice healthy way rather than the Maccy D's I would forever order on UberEats to my chemo bed.

I'm forever grateful to my BFF Becca for this gift she gave me, and whenever I find myself getting the sniffles I steal her chicken broth recipe and it quickly warms my tummy and my heart.

LAUREN MAHON
Girl vs Cancer

Ingredients

BROTH:

COCONUT OIL.

1kg CHICKEN - THIGHS plus DRUMSTICKS or WHOLE LEGS (on the bone for broth goodness).

1 BUTTERNUT SQUASH.

2 CARROTS.

2 BELL PEPPERS.

1 SCOTCH BONNET PEPPER (optional).

LARGE THUMB GINGER.

1 ONION.

5 CLOVES OF GARLIC.

4 SPRING ONIONS.

HANDFUL of THYME.

HANDFUL of PARSLEY.

2 tbsp PAPRIKA.

2 tbsp ALLSPICE or 3 PIMENTO BERRIES.

4 POTATOES.

BESTIE'S CHICKEN BROTH AND DUMPLINGS

DUMPLINGS:

2 cups of SELF-RAISING FLOUR.

1 pinch of SALT

Method

Melt a couple of tablespoons of coconut oil into a pan and brown off the chicken. Remove the chicken and set aside.

Add more oil into the pan if needed. Fry off onions, garlic, carrots and peppers. Once these have softened, grate in some ginger — the more the better as it's really good for the immune system.

Now add the chicken back in and stir. Sprinkle in parsley and thyme (they are fab for warding off colds) as well as paprika and either allspice or crushed pimento berries.

Next, add in chicken stock and bring to the boil. Turn down the heat to a simmer and let cook for as long as possible.

If you'd like the butternut squash to melt into and thicken the broth, add it at the beginning. If you'd like to have it chunky, add the squash with the potatoes about half an hour before the end.

For the dumplings, mix the flour with some cold water and salt to create a sticky dough. Roll into sausage shapes about 2—3cms long and place on top of the broth for the last 15—20 minutes.

The special ingredient is the Scotch Bonnet! If you only want a bit of heat cut a few slices of the skin and throw it in at any time. To achieve a deep spiciness, throw the whole pepper in the pot. But PLEASE remember to remove before serving. DO NOT let anyone eat it whole — they may turn purple!

GABBY LOGAN
Broadcaster and Presenter

This is a great recipe that my family love. It's my 'go to' when I am really up against it for time but want to feed the kids something nutritious and tasty. With a crisp salad, it's also perfect for a summer's evening of entertaining. And in winter, it's wonderful with a jacket potato.

I've always loved fruit with meat and the orange juice works a treat. The peaches need to be nicely chargrilled, and with the couscous, harissa and mint there's a lovely mixture of flavours. I hope you enjoy this as much as we do.

ORANGE CHICKEN

Ingredients
12 CHICKEN THIGHS (SKIN ON).
ENGLISH MUSTARD.
ORANGE JUICE.
BROWN SUGAR.
OLIVE OIL.

Accompaniments:
COUSCOUS (giant).
HARISSA to taste.
MINT.
GRILLED PEACHES.
Or
WILD RICE.
FRESH GREENS.

Method

Preheat your oven to 200°C, gas mark 6.

Take the chicken thighs and coat them in English mustard. Place them in a large dish and pour orange juice over them so the level reaches halfway up.

Dust the top of the chicken with brown sugar and finish with a drizzle of olive oil before placing in the oven.

Cook for 20 minutes, then take out of the oven and turn the chicken over. Baste with the orange juice, dust a bit more sugar on top and cook for another 20 minutes.

A TASTE OF HOME

SPRIG of MINT LEAVES.

CLOVE of GARLIC.

SALT and PEPPER for seasoning .

BLACK COTTON SQUARES (circa 10cm square).

STRING.

MACARONI.

PARMESAN.

TONI MINICHIELLO
Multiple Olympic and World Medal Winning Coach.

I came from a big Italian family with roots near Naples. Each of my parents had nine siblings. Life in rural Italy in the 1950s was tough, so most of the brothers and sisters travelled far and wide for employment. My mum moved to Sheffield with friends to work as a cook and my dad, who courted her by letter, came to join her later.

Dad worked shifts in the steel mills which meant that Sunday lunch was the one time we'd all sit down together. We'd get all the ingredients from a deli van which would drive round and visit all the Italian families so they could stock up on imported specialities.

To be honest, Sunday was an eating day full stop! I think it was the chance to reaffirm their decision to move away from poverty to England, whilst keeping a connection to their original home.

A mainstay of our Sunday eating marathons was my mum's Bolognese sauce served with macaroni.

Ingredients

500g BEEF or CHUCK STEAK
(ideally sourced from local butchers).

2 tbsp TOMATO PURÉE.

2 tins peeled PLUM TOMATOES.

Method

Take the beef or chuck steak, lay it out on a slab and using a wooden mallet (a rolling pin wrapped in tea towel will do) pummel and tenderise until it's thin and flat.

Cut into thick strips of circa 2–3cm, then season each strip generously on one side and sprinkle with mint leaves.

Roll up each strip and bundle into the cotton, tying with string (imagine miniature sleeping bags).

Heat a slug of olive oil in a pot or deep frying pan and fry the meat until brown.

Add garlic and once softened throw in the tomato puree along with the meat juices.

Remove the meat and add the peeled plum tomatoes. Bring to the boil and simmer.

Return the meat to the pot and allow to slow simmer for around 2–3 hours to ensure it is really tender and the flavour has permeated through.

You're then ready to serve up your sauce (unless of course you leave it overnight to cool and reheat it the next day like we did). You'll need to remove the cotton from the meat (easier when it's cool) but should find everything just crumbles away easily.

Mum used to give us mountains of macaroni, always al dente, which we'd scrape generous amounts of parmesan onto before the sauce was added. After that we'd usually eat a simple salad of lettuce, tomato and onion with a simple olive oil and vinegar dressing. I guess you'd call it peasant food — simple but hearty and healthy in equal measure.

CARRIE'S TOAD IN THE HOLE

Ingredients

125g PLAIN FLOUR.

1 tsp SALT.

2 EGGS.

300ml MILK.

2 tbsp LARD.

8 SAUSAGES

TONY ADAMS
Former Arsenal and England Football Captain

The seventies were, I am led to believe, not a gastronomic high-point in British culture. But down in Dagenham, in Foxland's Road where I was brought up, I wouldn't have had a clue. Because my mum's Toad in the Hole was clearly the Best Ever.

Mondays and Thursdays would mean late tea because getting to and from the Arsenal as a 13 year-old was quite a schlep. So on those days we would have the perennial favourite of beans on toast — probably not recipe-worthy! But on Saturdays. Oh Saturdays was toad-in-the-hole.

As a schoolboy at the Arsenal I would have a Saturday morning match, then my dad and I would go straight to watch the seniors in action. By the time we got home at 7pm, tea would be on the table and I would pile in before my mum and dad went to Bingo and my elder sister Sandra would babysit me. This routine carried on until I left home at 23. And probably still does without the babysitting...

Method

Turn the oven to 220°C.

Start with the batter. Mix the flour and salt in a bowl, make a hollow and add the eggs. Mix together and slowly add the milk. Whisk until not so lumpy.

Fry up the sausages until cooked through. Put the lard in the roasting tin and heat up until very hot (smoking a bit). Put the sausages in the roasting tin and pour over the batter.

Shove it all in the oven and bake for about 20–30 minutes.

I am assuming that nowadays lard is a no-no (I know my wife doesn't cook with it). She's also telling me to add onions and fry with the sausages, before adding in a slug of apple juice when they're pretty much ready to make them sweet and sticky. But that's not mum's...

Eat with peas! We never had ketchup — my dad would add brown sauce. But now I wouldn't eat it without mustard, ketchup, brown sauce — the whole caboodle.

GRANDMA HELEN'S MEAT AND POTATO PIE

Ingredients and Method

Brown some beef mincemeat in a small amount of olive oil in a pan.

Simmer with chopped potatoes, carrots, onions and a stock cube for about 40 minutes (and season).

Grease and line an ovenproof pie plate with (bought) shortcrust pastry, and spoon in the meat mixture.

Roll out the pastry for the top of the pie and place over the mince. Seal the edges and brush with milk or egg.

Bake in the oven and serve with potatoes and veg, having reserved some meat mix for the gravy.

VICTORIA DERBYSHIRE
Journalist and Broadcaster

Every week my mum would take us to my grandma's (her mum) for lunch. My grandma, Helen, lived in the next town to us, Bury, in a small bungalow with my grandad. Their house was warm and cosy, and it always smelled of home-made cooking.

Helen would make proper Lancashire fare — meat and potato pie and veg. It was absolutely delicious and incredibly comforting, particularly in the winter. My younger brother, sister and I adored the food and the ambience. It's got to be the easiest thing to make (although I didn't realise it back then).

SAM THOMAS
Gold Cup Winning Jockey

Being brought up in the countryside as children we were very much used to eating fresh meat and game, most of which was sourced locally or shot at one of our local shoots. As keen riders, Saturdays saw my sister and I usually attending our local hunt, the Monmouthshire, which would mean being on horseback for most of the day in typical Welsh cold and wet weather! When coming home exhausted there was nothing more comforting than the smell of mum's freshly cooked home food to warm us all up. And here it is...

MUM'S VENISON CASSEROLE

Ingredients

2 CARROTS, roughly chopped.

140g TURNIP or SWEDE, roughly chopped.

2 ONIONS, roughly chopped.

3 CELERY STICKS, roughly chopped.

OLIVE OIL and BUTTER, for frying.

1 GARLIC CLOVE, crushed.

1kg BONED LEG or SHOULDER of VENISON, cut into large chunks (or buy ready-cubed venison for stewing).

5 tbsp PLAIN FLOUR, seasoned with SALT and PEPPER.

2 tbsp REDCURRANT JELLY (or Rowan or Hawthorn Jelly).

450ml DRY RED WINE (Rioja is good).

450ml BEEF STOCK.

2 THYME SPRIGS.

1 BAY LEAF.

Method

Heat the oven to 180°C, fan 160°C, gas mark 4. Fry the vegetables in a little oil and butter in a heavy-based casserole for 4—5 mins until golden. Tip in the garlic and fry for a further minute, then set aside.

Put the venison into a plastic bag with seasoned flour and shake to coat. Add a little more oil and butter to the pan, then fry the venison over a high heat, stirring now and then, until well browned. Don't crowd the pan — cook in batches if necessary. Set aside with the vegetables.

Add the redcurrant jelly and wine to the pan, and bring to the boil, scraping up all the bits that have stuck to the bottom. Pour in the stock, then add the thyme, bay leaf, meat and vegetables. Season if you like and bring to the boil. Cover and transfer to the oven for about $1\frac{1}{2}$ hours or until tender. Remove from the oven and check the seasoning.

DR SARAH JARVIS, MBE
GP and Clinical Director of Patient.info

The recipe I've chosen is old-fashioned but is one of our standbys for a midweek meal for the family. It was one of my mother's favourites. My father was a keen vegetable gardener, and we always had fabulous fresh vegetables from the garden to go with every meal, but my parents definitely didn't hold with new-fangled ideas about meals without meat!

The smell of this meatloaf takes me back to my childhood, and it's a great way to make an economical main course with mince that's very different from the usual spaghetti bolognaise or cottage pie.

My mother died from cancer but had a really good death, for which I will always be grateful. In my 27 year career as a GP I have seen so many patients struggle, but have also witnessed the extraordinary difference Maggie's makes.

The patients in my practice are lucky enough to have a Maggie's Centre within minutes of their homes, and I have watched the change in my patients after they have been taken under Maggie's wing and have benefitted from the practical and emotional support they offer.

When we married, we decided to ask our guests to make a donation to Maggie's rather than giving wedding presents — so you could say we got married for Maggie's!

GRANDMA JOYCE'S MEATLOAF

Ingredients

500g LEAN MINCE.

250g BACK BACON, chopped.

1 LARGE ONION, finely chopped.

3 tbsp CHOPPED PARSLEY.

1 EGG, beaten.

1 tsp SALT.

2 tsp GROUND PEPPER.

100g FRESH WHOLEMEAL BREADCRUMBS.

DRIED BREADCRUMBS for coating.

Method

Preheat oven to 200°C, fan 180°C. Mix all ingredients in a large bowl. Form into a single sausage shape, wrap tightly in tin foil and secure the ends.

Bake on a baking tray for 1 hour, turning over half way through.

Remove from foil, brush with escaped juices and turn in dried breadcrumbs, pressing them in firmly.

Serve hot with new potatoes and vegetables or cold with hot crusty bread and salad.

MY MUM'S SAUSAGE ROAST

100g dry BREADCRUMBS.

50g SOFT BUTTER.

ZEST of 1 LEMON.

1 tbsp whole toasted FENNEL SEEDS.

1 tsp dry CHILLI FLAKES.

3 tbsp chopped FRESH PARSLEY.

100ml WHITE WINE.

TOM KERRIDGE
Owner of The Hand and Flowers

This is my first real taste of cooking that I remember and one that means so much to me. Money was short when I was young. My brother and I were growing lads and my mum was working very hard to bring us up as best she could as a single parent. We never felt that we went without and this is an example of her great vision. We could have a rolled sausage meat as a 'roast' instead of a more expensive joint of meat, but served with all the trimmings. Fantastic! It must be where my love of sausages comes from.

Ingredients

1kg minced PORK SHOULDER.

300g minced PORK BELLY.

15g TABLE SALT.

1 tbsp toasted FENNEL SEEDS, ground to a powder.

2 tsp dry OREGANO.

3 cloves of GRATED GARLIC.

1 tsp CAYENNE PEPPER.

2 dry BAY LEAVES, ground to a powder.

Method

Place the minced pork shoulder and pork belly into a large mixing bowl. Add the table salt, ground fennel seeds, dry oregano, garlic, cayenne pepper and the ground bay leaves. Get your hands in and start to work the mix together. You need to knead this like a bread dough and work it for a least 5 minutes. This helps to work and stretch the proteins and forms a tighter mix that will hold its shape better. After this time, add the breadcrumbs, whole fennel seeds, dry chilli flakes, white wine and the chopped fresh parsley. Mix together with your hands.

Roll a large sheet of tin foil on to a surface and rub it with soft butter. Place the sausage meat onto the foil in the shape of a log. Try to make it tight together so there are no gaps. Once you have made a giant sausage, roll the tin foil over the top and secure the ends tightly, like a Christmas cracker. Place the roll into the fridge to firm up for at least 2 hours but preferably overnight.

Pre-heat the oven at 180°C and take the tin foil roll out of the fridge and place onto a flat baking tray. Roast in the oven for 25–30 minutes, after this time, unravel the tin foil and place the sausage back into the oven and roast for a further minute or so until it goes a golden brown roasted colour. It is now ready to serve with all of your normal vegetable roast garnish or some braised white beans or anything else that you fancy!

MAMAN BLANC'S WATERCRESS SOUP

SERVES 8.

Ingredients

20g / 1 tbsp BUTTER, UNSALTED.

100g / ½ ONION, FINELY CHOPPED.

400g / 4 LARGE BUNCHES WATERCRESS, *stalks removed.

100g / 1 HANDFUL SPINACH, washed and picked.

8g / 8 pinches SEA SALT.

1g / 2 PINCHES PEPPER, BLACK, freshly ground.

750ml WATER, BOILING.**

750ml ICE.***

RAYMOND BLANC, OBE

I was taught this dish by my mother. Maman never used stock for soups, she followed her belief that the main ingredients should provide enough flavour so this recipe is no exception to that rule. Today, the gardeners grow watercress at Belmond Le Manoir aux Quat'Saisons in polytunnels to provide the kitchen and The Raymond Blanc Cookery School with the freshest ingredients.

This simple soup brings out all the qualities of watercress; fresh, tangy and peppery. It can be made one day in advance, but it is always better when it is made just before serving.

Method

On a low heat, sweeten the onion in the butter until softened and translucent. Turn up the heat, add the watercress and spinach and wilt for two minutes. Add the water (boiling), season with the sea salt and pepper, and quick boil for two minutes. Add the ice to stop the cooking and blend in a liquidiser until very smooth. Reheat, taste and correct the seasoning if required. Serve immediately, piping hot, in a large soup tureen.

Chef's Notes

*According to the variety, the watercress may vary in its strength of flavour. If your watercress is very peppery, cut off the entire stalk, but if it is mild, keep some of the stalk.

**The boiling water speeds up the making of the soup and retains the colour and flavour of the watercress.

***The ice stops the cooking, which will keep the vivid colour, the flavour and the nutrients. Reheat the soup at the last moment for the same reasons.

Variations

As a good Frenchman, I would be tempted to add a clove of pureed garlic or flakes of toasted garlic to the soup.

A tablespoon of Greek yoghurt would be a nice addition.

A squeeze of lemon juice added at the last moment would heighten the flavour of the watercress, but add at the last minute or it will discolour the watercress.

RUFUS HOUND
World's Greatest Keeper of
Secrets and International Assasin.

(SERVES A NORMAL FAMILY FOR DAYS or
2 REALLY HUNGRY MEDIUM-SIZE SHEEP STEALERS).

Ingredients

1 SWEDE.

2 TURNIPS.

3 LARGE CARROTS.

4 Jacket potato size POTATOES.

2 LEEKS.

1 PARSNIP.

300g NECK OF LAMB.

1 BOTTLE (190ml) OF MUSHROOM KETCHUP
(Geo Watkins or something similar to that).

2–5 LITRES of COLD WATER.

¾ MUG of RED LENTILS.

¾ MUG of SPLIT PEAS.

A little bit of PLAIN FLOUR.

A splash of VEGETABLE OIL/ knob of BUTTER.

SALT and PEPPER.

TOOLS:

PRESSURE COOKER.

MANDOLIN SLICER / NINJA-STYLE KNIFE SKILLS

BIG SPOON.

BRAVEHEART OST (on vinyl if hipster).

FOR THE CHEESE ON TOAST:

The sort of CHEESE that makes the
top of your mouth itch.

THE SORT OF BREAD that makes
Paul Hollywood drool.

One side of my family came from Dundee, a place where they speak mainly in the kind of Scottish accent often mistaken for Klingon. They were a simple people (mainly alcoholics, sheep rustlers and the inventor of golf) who would make up vast batches of this hearty, filling soup. My brother and I were raised on it. My grandma made it for us every time we saw her. It's one of just two things my Dad knows how to cook. If you were to cut any of my tribe, this is the stuff that would come pouring out.

Cut to 2006. With its significant place in my life, and its familial provenance beyond reproach, I felt I had reached the point when I was entitled to THE RECIPE. To my mind, I expected some kind of ceremony. A kilted man, stripped to the waist, yet somehow also hooded, would call me to a bubbling altar. Ghosts of my forebears would hold aloft flaming bagpipes whilst chanting "cumaibh faire fhad 'sa gheibh mi na caoraich seo a-steach don bhan" in varying harmonious monotones. A scroll written on purest Harris Tweed would be produced and I would swear an oath of secrecy before being allowed to gaze upon its contents. Ceremony complete, I would make a batch of soup for all present, and as my offering touched their lips, the bagpipes would fanfare, the hooded man would nod, and I would have been accepted as a true Brother of the Broth.

So, imagine my surprise when my Dad said "There's no recipe, son. You just stick a load of lamb and veg in a pressure cooker and try not to screw it up." I badgered him that there must be a bit more to it than that, and he did eventually provide me with his version of Family Soup (as it has forever been known to me), but he was at great pains to point out that everyone who has ever made it has changed what's in it, so it's less of a recipe and more of a concept. The thing his recipe did reveal was that there was more salt in his version than doctors advise you eat over the course of a lifetime, so that was my first change, salt out, mushroom ketchup in (it's got a tangy saltiness that I like. If you don't you can leave it out and just add a small fistful of sea salt instead).

The second change has more to do with my wife than me. My wife has always made cheese on toast to go with soup. Don't ask me why — she's just a savage, I guess. However, the expectation that any bowl of Bouillon, any porringer of Pozole, any crock of cockaleeky come accompanied by dairy on carbs has been inherited by my children so I offer it here as they'll kill me if I don't. Also, my wife always adds Sriracha to hers, but as I hope you realise by now, she is an awful woman with no respect for tradition, my heritage or basic human decency. Anyway, here's the recipe. Do what you want with it. I know I have.

FAMILY SOUP

Method

Take all the veg, peel and divide into two ($\frac{1}{2}$ a swede, 1 turnip, $1\frac{1}{2}$ carrots etc). Using a mandolin slicer (or coarser side of a grater, I guess) shred one half of the veg. Using a knife, chop the other half of the veg into chunks the size of half a Cadbury's Wispa. Make the lamb be in chunks of the same size, using your mind laser / raw strength / also the knife. Throw some salt and pepper into a small plate of plain flour, then toss the lamb chunks in the salty-peppery flour until they're well-coated. Get your pressure cooker on the hob. Stick a bit of oil / your knob of butter in the bottom of it and get it hot but not smoking. If that happens you've burnt literally the first thing you've had to do in this recipe. Maybe step away and have a think if cooking's really for you, yeah?

Providing you've not messed up that last bit, add your floury lamb chunks. Keep poking them about until they're brown all over, then take them out. You could do this bit in a separate pan, I suppose, but it's just more washing up. Put the pressure cooker back on the heat. Add about a litre of water, or if you're a Brexit fan who wants to go back to imperial measurements, 1.759754 pints. Now, most pressure cookers come with a bit that keeps what's inside the pot from sitting directly on the cooker's bottom. From what I can work out from Wikipedia, it seems to be meant for steaming things, but I've never used mine for that. I stick mine in the water at this stage so that nothing sticks to the bottom of the pan and burns. If that happens the whole soup becomes bitter — so try to avoid it.

Now bung all of the veg and lamb in the pan. Add more water, until the ingredients are just submerged. Add the mushroom ketchup. How much depends on how much you like mushroom ketchup. I'd say you want no less than 100ml. I use about 150ml. Give it a stir. Try and get it so all the lentils don't sink straight to the bottom. Psyche! They're always going to — I can't believe you fell for that! Get it so the whole thing is steaming hot. Stick the lid on your pressure cooker and cook the heck out of it. With about five minutes to go until you're ready to serve it up, make an absolute ton of cheese on toast, enough that everyone who's eating gets at least two slices each. Shout at wife as she puts Sriracha Hot Sauce on the table, because if you're just going to add that to it Beth, why did I even bother cooking this, when all you'll taste is the hot sauce and NOT THE ACTUAL SOUP I WAS RAISED ON. Start Braveheart soundtrack. Serve. Eat.

RACHEL RILEY
TV Presenter

I'll start by explaining my parents are in a mixed marriage — my Mum's Jewish and my Dad's Manchester United. We've worshipped the Reds far more often than I can ever claim to have gone to shul but I'm still proud of both heritages and I love the Jewish food I was brought up on.

Mum's a proper Jewish Mum in that she's a feeder and puts on a great spread of traditional food like bagels (beigels in our house) and smoked salmon for the family when they come over. It always made me laugh though, that in our non-religious family, every year we'd sit down to our Christmas dinner with a starter of Jewish style chicken soup, with the chicken swapped out for the Christmas turkey!

It was my Grandad (my Zada's) favourite, and now he's no longer with us, remembering him ask for seconds every year holds an even more special memory for me.

JEWISH CHRISTMAS TURKEY SOUP

Ingredients and Method

Put two sets of turkey giblets in a pressure cooker.

Add 2 large sliced onions.

Add around 4 large carrots — cut them into quarters lengthways, then cut the lenghs in half.

Add 3–4 sticks of celery cut into 2 inch pieces.

Add 2–3 chicken stock cubes

Put in around 4 pints of water and season with some pepper.

Put the lid on the pressure cooker and steam on high for around 20 minutes.

Take the giblets out before serving (unless you like the liver).

That's it innit! Eat soup!

SWEET

SUPER BREAKFAST

Method

Fill a small to medium size saucepan with a mix of water and hemp / almond milk. Bring almost to the boil. Add the oats and let them cook for 2 minutes while stirring. Finally, add the raspberries, blueberries, almonds, shredded coconut, chia seeds and spirulina. Stir in gently then serve.

MORE ABOUT THE INGREDIENTS AND THEIR BENEFITS...

SPIRULINA will turn your oats green, do not be alarmed! Spirulina is a super food and one of the best things you can eat. This natural algae is very high in essential amino acids, protein, iron, B vitamins and antioxidants.

HEMP MILK should not be feared but embraced. One glass provides a substantial dose of omega-3; vitamins A, E, B12, and D; 10 essential amino acids; and about half the recommended daily calcium intake. And all without cholesterol or sugar.

ALMONDS aren't cheap but a 2018 study by the BBC ranked the almond top of the 100 Greatest Foods. Extremely high in mono-saturated fats, antioxidants, vitamin E and B2, manganese, magnesium, fibre and protein, almonds may also reduce blood sugar, blood pressure and cholesterol.

WILLIAM MOSELEY
Actor, *The Chronicles of Narnia* Films & *The Royals*.

This is a breakfast I make almost every morning. It's a combined carbohydrate recipe which provides a slow release of energy throughout the day. If you exercise, then this is for you. It also makes the porridge fun.

Though this is quite in-depth for a bowl of porridge, I think there are some good things within the recipe and it should take no longer than 5 minutes to make. Your day will be set up and you'll know that you have done something good yourself before 9am. I hope you enjoy it!

Ingredients

OATS — as needed.

1 glass ALMOND or HEMP MILK.

1 glass WATER.

¼ cup RASPBERRIES.

¼ cup BLUEBERRIES.

¼ cup ALMONDS.

3 tbsp shredded COCONUT.

2 tbsp CHIA SEEDS.

1 tbsp SPIRULINA.

FAMILY PANCAKES

Ingredients

150g PLAIN FLOUR.

2 EGGS.

450ml MILK.

DROP of VANILLA ESSENCE.

OIL for cooking.

RICHARD SCUDAMORE
Excecutive Chairman of
The Premier League.

My mother always used to make pancakes on Shrove Tuesday, never on any other day of the year. When I was about ten years old I started to make my own and found they tasted good on other days too. I've always made my own children pancakes from as young as they could eat them and it has become a Sunday morning tradition in our house.

The children are a little older now: Jamie 30, Chloe 27, Paddy 16, Ned and Lara 13 — but I still make the pancakes. The eldest two are a little more adventurous, Paddy just likes them plain with sugar and lemon, Ned smothers his in Nutella.

My party piece is the teddy bear. Make a round pancake, save some batter in the ladle to create two ears, then use sultanas to form eyes and a mouth. It's still guaranteed to make Lara smile. Her friends, on sleepovers since she was about seven, rather affectionately still call me Pancake Man. The innocence of youth is rather lost on the boys now, they say I've always been a tosser.

Method

Sieve the flour into a bowl and add the eggs. Add half the milk and whisk into a thick batter. Add the tiniest drop of vanilla essence and then slowly add more milk, whisking as you go until there is a very smooth batter.

Heat a very shallow frying pan or special omelette/pancake pan until very hot. Baste with oil, just enough to prevent sticking — not too much or you will fry the batter.

Ladle in enough batter to create a circular pancake. When you see the batter solidify, use a spatula to loosen the edges and toss the pancake. After a little practice you will be able to judge how long is needed to produce perfect golden brown pancakes on both sides.

Add caster sugar and lemon juice before serving. Alternatively, add all sorts of other nice things into the wet batter such as sliced bananas, blueberries, sultanas, raisins, chocolate chips or Nutella. Create your own favourites. Enjoy.

MICHAEL PERRY
Mr Plant Geek.

I was always a busy kid — whether that was growing herbs in the garden or trying out new recipes in the kitchen (as long as my Mum knew I would clear up afterwards) and I picked up this lavender recipe from one of my favourite childhood books: *Jekka's Complete Book of Herbs*. I was quite an entrepreneur as a teenager too, so was even selling small packs of lavender biscuits at the local WI markets!

LAVENDER BISCUITS

Ingredients
15g BUTTER, unsalted.

170g CASTER SUGAR.

1 EGG YOLK.

2 tbsp LEMON JUICE, fresh.

1 tbsp ZEST of LEMON.

340g PLAIN FLOUR.

120g ARROWROOT POWDER.

60g dried LAVENDER BLOSSOMS.

PINCH of SALT

Method

Cream the butter and sugar, then add the egg yolk, lemon juice and zest. Stir to mix.

Add the flour and arrowroot with the lavender blossoms and a pinch of salt. Stir until the mix holds together well.

Remove from the bowl and wrap in greaseproof paper. Chill the dough for 30 minutes, or until firm. Preheat the oven to 170°C.

Slice into $\frac{1}{4}$ inch wide biscuits and place on a greased baking sheet, with an inch gap between each.

Bake for 25–30 minutes, checking after 25 minutes.

Cool on the sheet, then move to a cooling rack.

POOR KNIGHT'S PUDDING

Ingredients

PER PERSON.

2 SLICES of good quality WHITE BREAD.

RASBERRY JAM.

BUTTER.

A splash of SUNFLOWER OIL.

DOUBLE CREAM or CLOTTED CREAM.

SOPHIE GRIGSON
Principle of Sophie's
Cooking School and
British Cooking, Oxford

Method

Make a jam sandwich with the bread, raspberry and a little butter. Cut off the crusts if you are feeling very fancy.

Melt a big knob of butter with a dash of sunflower oil in a frying pan over a medium heat. Fry the sandwich until golden brown on both sides. Serve hot, with cream

When my mother was a little girl, she and her sister were often taken to tea with their grandmother. There was always a mountainous heap of raspberry jam sandwiches on the table, far, far more than they could possibly eat. Not a question of generosity or over-catering. My great grandma Barclay just adored Poor Knight's Pudding — left over jam sandwiches fried up in plenty of butter, and served crisp and golden brown outside, tenderly scarlet at heart, with a slick of cream.

Despite, or perhaps because of her indulgence, she lived well into her nineties. Family legend has it that she was a hypochondriac, and took to her bed for the last 20 years of her life, which may explain why I have no memories of her at all. Her favourite pudding, however, lives on in the family repertoire. My mother made it for me, sometimes sandwiching fresh raspberries and sugar between the slices of bread, instead of jam. I fried up jam sandwiches as a treat for my children when they were young. So that's at least five generations of Poor Knight's Pudding — and time for plenty more ahead.

MARMITE RICE PUDDING MUM'S WAY

Ingredients

50g SHORT GRAIN PUDDING RICE.

1 PINT GOLD TOP MILK.

25g SUGAR.

10ml MELTED BUTTER.

½ tsp GRATED NUTMEG

KATE STARKEY
Mother and Owner
of Cheltenham Maman

Don't panic guys, there is no Marmite in the rice pudding — that would quite clearly be madness. But much like Marmite, rice pudding is one of those things that I think you either love or hate. For me, piercing the nutmeg enhanced skin on the top of one of my Mum's baked rice puddings evokes a memory of family, safety and cosy afternoons pottering at a home I loved dearly.

To my husband on the other hand, the mere mention of rice pudding is enough to have him running from the table and it's for that reason that I haven't made or sampled this recipe in a very very long time. Just writing this down is making me salivate — I just love it.

I'd be fascinated to know your thoughts on this dish — is it love or hate?

Method

Soak the rice in the cold milk for two hours. Then heat the oven to 150°C, gas mark 2.

Put the milk, rice, sugar and butter in a deep 600ml baking dish. Stir well, sprinkle with the nutmeg and place in the lower half of a preheated oven for 2–2½ hours. Stir every half hour. Serve!

TOM HETHERINGTON
Architect. Great British Bake Off 08. Maggie's Fundraiser.

When I was a child, my siblings and I would spend hours in the kitchen with our mother. As a result, we all love to cook and bake. Some of my happiest memories are of baking in the kitchen, making one hell of a mess, and putting whatever we had made into the oven. Whilst it would cool we'd play in the garden, and then come back in and enjoy a slice of something delicious. It was an idyllic time, and many summers were spent repeating this. This cake celebrates those beautiful, fresh days, where the sun shines and the birds sing. Sadly, those days can't be guaranteed in Britain, though the sharp lemon flavour can help make it feel as though it's bright outside.

Ingredients

250g SOFT SALTED BUTTER.

250g SUGAR + 1 tbsp.

250g SELF RAISING FLOUR + 1 tbsp.

3 large LEMONS, zested and juiced.

5 LARGE EGGS room temperature, beaten PLUS up to 50ml of MILK.

1½ tsp BAKING POWDER.

PINCH of SALT.

300g BLUEBERRIES.

LEMON AND BLUEBERRY CAKE

ICING:

500g ICING SUGAR.

3 tsp LEMON ESSENCE.

125g FULL FAT CREAM CHEESE.

60g soft SALTED BUTTER.

ZEST of 1 LEMON, for decoration

Method

Heat your oven to 170°C fan. Grease and line two 8 inch round spring-form cake tins.

Cream together butter and sugar until pale and creamy. Mix in the zest, along with the eggs adding one third of the eggs at a time. Between each addition of eggs add two tablespoons of the flour, this is to stop the mixture from curdling.

Sieve together the baking powder and flour, before mixing this into the other ingredients — try not to overwork the batter or it will be tough. Mix until it is just combined. This is when you might need to add some milk — the mixture should not be too stiff.

Separately, mix the blueberries with the single tablespoon of flour. Lightly fold the blueberries into the cake mixture, splitting the mixture between the two tins. Bake in the oven for 35–40 minutes until the cakes spring back when lightly touched and a skewer comes out clean when inserted.*

Mix the lemon juice and one tablespoon of sugar together. Whilst the cakes are still warm, poke holes all over their tops with a skewer*. Pour the lemon syrup over the cakes — splitting it equally between the two. Allow the cakes to cool in their tins before removing, so the syrup can absorb.

To make the icing, beat together the butter, cream cheese and one third of the icing sugar. Add the lemon essence and the remaining icing sugar, and beat until light and fluffy.

To assemble, spread half of the icing on one cake, top with the other cake, and then the remaining icing. Use a spoon and spin the cake to make a swirl pattern on the top. Using a zester, cut long curls of the lemon skin to decorate the top of the cake. Serve!

*Tip: if you don't have a cake skewer, raw spaghetti works well too.

HERMIONE NORRIS
Actress

Enjoyed by young and not so young and truly delicious for afternoon tea or dessert.

Ingredients

225g STORK CAKE MARGARINE (soft).

225g CASTER SUGAR.

225g sifted SELF-RAISING FLOUR.

2 tsp BAKING POWDER.

4 LARGE EGGS.

FOR THE FILLING AND TO DECORATE:

1 PINT of DOUBLE CREAM.

2 SMALL or 1 LARGE PUNNET OF STRAWBERRIES or RASPBERRIES or a mixture of both using the raspberries for the middle and the strawberries for the top.

MY MOTHER'S STRAWBERRY (OR RASPBERRY) CAKE

Method

Before measuring the ingredients, grease and line 2 loose-bottom 8-inch sponge tins with greaseproof paper. Heat the oven to gas mark 4.

Place all the measured ingredients into a large bowl and beat for no more than 2 minutes. I always use an electric hand whisk starting on number one and increasing to three as the mixture softens and blends.

Divide the mixture equally between the two prepared tins. Place in the centre of the oven and bake for 25 minutes until golden and risen. The tops should spring back when pressed with a finger.

Remove from the oven and allow to cool in the tins for a few minutes. Loosen the cakes by carefully placing a knife around the edge, then remove the cakes from the tins and place on a wire rack to cool completely.

Place one cake top downwards on a serving plate and cover with a thin layer of whipped double cream. Then cover with halved strawberries or raspberries.

Dust with a fine dusting of icing sugar and then apply a second layer of cream to cover the fruit. (Do not use too much icing sugar or the flavour will be too sweet).

Place the second sponge on top of the first and cover it with cream followed by whole or halved raspberries or strawberries. Finally, sprinkle a fine dusting of icing sugar over the fruit. Serve sliced.

This cake will last for up to 3 days in the fridge – either in a cake tin or carefully wrapped in tin foil.

MARTHA KEARNEY
Broadcaster

The secret ingredient in this cake is honey from my own bees so it brings back happy memories of sunny days and sticky kitchens after extracting honey from the beeswax.

I created it for the Comic Relief Great British Bake Off which is why the bees had red noses. You can also paint their stripes with melted chocolate. You might not need all the butter icing so do feel free to adapt. I also now use crushed pistachio nuts to create a grass effect around the cake.

Ingredients

400g/14oz BUTTER, softened.

400g/14oz SUGAR.

2 tbsp HONEY.

2 LEMONS, zest only.

7 free-range EGGS (preferably organic).

400g/14oz SELF-RAISING FLOUR, sifted.

FOR THE DECORATION:

1kg/2LB 4oz BUTTER, softened.

1.5kg/3lb 5oz ICING SUGAR, sifted.

LEMON JUICE.

1 tbsp HONEY, or to taste.

GOLDEN-YELLOW COLOURING
- rather than lemon.

SMALL AMOUNTS of READY-TO-ROLL
FONDANT ICING in YELLOW, BLACK,
RED AND WHITE.

25g/1oz FLAKED ALMONDS.

250g/9oz ready-to-roll GREEN FONDANT ICING.

Method

1. Preheat oven to 180°C, 350°F, gas mark 4. Grease and line a 15cm / 6in cake tin and a 18cm / 7in cake tin. Grease a 15cm / 6in oven-proof glass bowl or similar. Cut out a small circle of baking paper to fit in the bottom of the bowl. Flour the sides.

2. Cream the butter and sugar until it is very pale, light and fluffy. Beat in the lemon zest and honey.

3. Add the eggs slowly plus a little flour if the batter looks like it may curdle. Fold in the remaining flour with a large metal spoon.

4. Divide the mixture between the cake tins and the oven-proof bowl.

5. Bake for 40–50 minutes, checking the smaller cakes after 30 minutes. The cakes are done when a skewer inserted into the centre of the cake comes out clean.

HIVE CAKE

Method

6. Remove from the oven and cool in the tins for 10 minutes before turning out onto a wire rack to cool completely. Remove the baking paper carefully.

7. For the decoration, beat the softened butter in a free-standing mixer for 5–8 minutes until very light and soft. Add the icing sugar in gradually, beating all the time, until it is all incorporated. Loosen this buttercream icing mixture with the lemon juice and flavour with honey, to taste. Beat the golden-yellow food colouring into the buttercream icing to achieve your desired shade.

8. Dust the work surface with icing sugar. Knead the yellow fondant icing until soft and pliable, then roll small amounts into rugby balls to form the body of the bees. Knead the black icing until soft and roll out on the dusted work surface into very thin ropes to create stripes. Brush the bees very lightly with water and stick on the stripes. Roll tiny balls of red for noses (if you wish), and little balls of white with black dots for eyes. Stick these on with a very little water. Push two slices of almond into each bee for wings. Set aside to dry.

9. Roll out the white fondant icing and use a daisy cutter to cut out white flowers. Cut small circles from the yellow fondant for the centres of the daisies. Set aside to dry.

10. Roll out the green fondant icing to cover the cake board.

11. Place the largest cake on the green lined cake board. Spread a layer of the buttercream on the top, then top with the smaller cake. Spread a little more buttercream on the top and then finish with the round bowl cake.

12. Spread a thin layer of buttercream all over the outside of the cake. Set aside to harden (preferably in the fridge) for 10–15 minutes.

13. Transfer the remaining buttercream to a piping bag fitted with a plain 2cm / ¾in nozzle. Pipe the icing around the outside of the cake in concentric circles to create a hive shape. On the top, pipe a spiral and smooth with a palette knife.

14. Place a few bees on skewers or cocktail sticks and stick into the cake. Attach other bees directly to the hive. Place daisies on the cake and on the green board.

Ingredients

FOR THE CAKE:

250g PLAIN FOUR.

1½ tsp BAKING POWDER.

½ tsp BICARBONATE of SODA.

¼ tsp SALT.

200ml BUTTERMILK.

1½ tsp VANILLA EXTRACT.

125g SOFT UNSALTED BUTTER.

225g CASTER SUGAR.

3 LARGE EGGS.

FOR THE ICING:

300g BUTTER.

700g ICING SUGAR, sieved.

1 tsp VANILLA EXTRACT.

2 tbsp MILK.

OPTIONAL FILLING:

4–6 tbsp of your favourite JAM.

AMBER'S VANILLA BUTTERMILK CAKE

within months of the babies' birth. In a corner of a local restaurant, as the same wonderful friends from the baby shower gathered around and sung Happy Birthday, Amber stood smiling in front of me holding a cake. I looked at her, my eyes widening. She could read my thoughts.

Is it? Is it really? Oh, tell me it is! "It's the buttermilk cake, darling. I made it especially." It was happy adrenaline that night. Not the other kind. So that night I ate two slices. And life felt good.

EMMA CAMPBELL
Author of *All that Followed — A Story of Cancer, Kids & the Fear of Leaving Too Soon.*

Oh sugar, wonderful, sweet, sublime sugar. It's always been a dangerous love affair. Never more so than in the months leading up to the birth of my triplets back in 2009 when I seemed to survive on little more than endless packets of chocolate digestives dunked into hot, sweet tea. My friend Amber, along with more incredible pals, threw me an epic baby shower. There were cards, gifts, personalised bobbly hats and bibs and there was cake. Oh, so much cake.

But as everyone tucked in on that sunny but cold November morning, as they piled their plates high with a selection of warm, buttery, melt in the mouth delights, I stood back. You see I wasn't in a great place that day. I'd just separated from the babies' father after a dreadful few months and the future felt terrifying. So, running on adrenaline, my appetite was the first to suffer. Until, that is, Amber appeared with her famous Vanilla Buttermilk Cake complete with Buttermilk icing. I stepped forward and took a slice. A huge slice. And tucked straight into the icing. Oh, the icing! Thick, soft and oh, so sweet. Too sweet for some but not for me, never for me.

Eighteen months later, the triplets now sixteen months old and my eldest aged eight, Amber came up trumps once more. It was my fortieth birthday and I was reeling from a brutal battle with breast cancer, the diagnosis coming

Method

Line and grease two 18cm round sandwich tins.
Preheat your oven to 180°C, gas mark 4.

In one bowl, sift the flour, baking powder, bicarbonate of soda and salt together.

Pour the buttermilk into a jug and stir in the vanilla extract.

In another bowl, cream the butter and sugar together with an electric mixer at a medium speed until light and fluffy. Continue to mix at a reduced speed adding the eggs one at a time and beating for approximately 30 seconds after each egg.

Add alternating amounts of the flour mixture and the vanilla buttermilk mixture and blend well after each addition. This should take between three and five minutes.

Pour the mixture into the prepared sandwich tins and cook for approximately 30 minutes. The cake should begin to shrink away from the sides and a cake tester should come out clean.

Place the tins on a wire rack for 10 minutes before taking out the cakes to let cool completely.

The easiest way to make the buttermilk icing is to place the icing sugar into a food processor and blitz until completely smooth. This removes the need to sieve. Then add the remaining ingredients and process until you have a lovely, smooth creamy icing.

Sandwich the cakes together, with or without the optional jam, then proceed to cover the entire cake with the vanilla buttercream icing, smoothing as you go with a wet palette knife.

CAROLE CARTER
Maggie's West London Visitor

I first made these recipes about 40 years ago while taking a Cordon Bleu course and both of them became great favourites with the family over the years. Since my cancer diagnosis, I lost all interest in cooking until I came to Maggie's when I began making cakes for everyone.

Recently, I made the roulade for Dave (a fellow Centre visitor), my first one for a long time, which he enjoyed. So I guess I haven't lost my touch.

PINEAPPLE CHEESECAKE

Ingredients

SMALL PACKET of DIGESTIVE BISCUITS.

2oz BUTTER.

8oz CURD CHEESE or LOW FAT CHEESE.

1 CARTON of SOURED CREAM.

2 EGGS.

1 TIN of CRUSHED PINEAPPLE.

2–3oz CASTER SUGAR.

A SQUEEZE of LEMON JUICE.

1½ tsp VANILLA ESSENCE.

Method

Crush the biscuits in the melted butter and line an 8-inch flan tin.

Mix curd cheese, beaten eggs and drained pineapple.
Add half a teaspoon of vanilla essence and a squeeze of lemon juice. Pour the mixture into the lined flan tin and bake for 25 minutes at 375°F, 190°C, gas mark 5.
Leave to cool for one hour.

For the topping; mix the soured cream and caster sugar, adding one teaspoon of vanilla essence and a little lemon juice. Pour onto the cooked base, then cook for a further 10 minutes at the same oven temperature.

This is an especially refreshing cheesecake!

FOR THE LOVE OF TRIFLE

On the assumption that the parents wouldn't have a clue how much was left from the previous night, and the fact that as long as we were quiet and let them sleep in, we could tidy up the trifle bowl. We would take two dessert spoons and dig in.

Sunday mornings to this day are all about trifle. To lie on the sofa with a coffee and a sherry trifle is just pure nostalgia. Breakfast trifle is a delicacy not to be missed out on. My Mum's Secret Trifle Recipe probably doesn't do her cooking skills justice but for me it is all about the memory of such a happy childhood.

CAREY WHITE
alias MYLEGOMAN
Social Food Blogger @mylegoman

If you say trifle to me, I instantly light up and smile. For me trifle is a better invention than sliced bread, it is my comfort food, my childhood and now it's beginning to define me.

My Mum was an exceptional cook, she seemed to be able to effortlessly whip up a three course meal with nothing but an egg and half a jar of mayo in the fridge. My Dad united the troops with our family motto: "Suffer the main course to get to the pudding". And together they were a pretty awesome entertaining double act, hosting dinner parties for friends and family most weekends.

It was the 1970s and they were on trend, Mateus Rose, dessert trolley, Abba on vinyl. My brother and I were dispatched to our rooms as the guests arrived. The lounge door shut as my Dad poured cheap Spanish gin from a Gordon's bottle and added an ice cube from his pineapple shaped plastic ice bucket.

The next morning my brother and I would wake up to a quiet house. Both of us would convene in the kitchen in pajamas, shut the sliding door and then stand back in amazement as the fridge door was opened and the light came on! The remains of the dessert trolley were covered in cling film, and on the bottom shelf of the fridge was the cut glass trifle bowl.

Ingredients & Method:

Split trifle sponge cakes and butter them with raspberry jam. Sandwich together and cut them into 2 cm slices.

Organise a layer of the trifle sponges at the bottom of a huge trifle bowl.

Pour over raspberries from a tin. Perhaps add some fresh raspberries if they are available.

Add a very generous slug of sherry and a little raspberry juice to ensure the trifle sponges are soaked but not soggy.

Make up some Bird's custard. Increase the amount of custard powder to ensure the custard will set firmly. Pour the custard over the trifle sponges.

Leave in the fridge to set.

Whip up double cream with a little icing sugar and vanilla essence.

Smooth on the cream and pipe some blobs around the outside.

Decorate the top of the trifle with some diamond cut angelica and glace cherries to get the 1970s look. If trying for the classy look, go for some ratafia biscuits crushed around the outside.

In my mum's trifle world, jelly, blancmange and hundreds and thousands are simply not acceptable. However a trifle is all about personal choice so go with whatever makes you smile.

RASPBERRY AND AMARETTI TRIFLE

As my Christmases have passed I have re-created and tweaked this recipe as best I can and have now settled on an equally boozy and indulgent dessert which is reserved for Boxing Day. Having it just once a year makes it all the more special and every time I make it, I think of my Gan Gan, Mary.

Ingredients

80g TRIFLE SPONGES.

100g AMARETTI BISCUITS.

300g TINNED RASPBERRIES (drained).

300g FRESH RASPBERRIES.

3 tbsp AMARETTO LIQUEUR.

250g MASCARPONE.

500g FRESH CUSTARD.

300ml DOUBLE CREAM.

GOOD QUALITY DARK CHOCOLATE
for decoration.

Method

Roughly cut the trifle sponges into quarters and arrange in the bottom of your bowl (you can make individual trifles in glasses if you prefer — this amount should make 6–8).

Crumble the amaretti biscuits over the sponge and add the drained tinned raspberries and fresh raspberries (keeping a few aside for decoration).

Sprinkle 3 tablespoons of amaretto over the top.

Combine the mascarpone and fresh custard in a separate bowl, mixing it until smooth. Pour over the raspberries.

Whip the double cream until it forms soft peaks. Spoon over the mascarpone/custard mixture and spread evenly.

Grate the dark chocolate over the top of the trifle and add the remainder of the raspberries for decoration.

FLORA MOUNTFORD
Owner of Violet & Percy

My Grandma's kitchen was a magical place when I was growing up — full of well-thumbed recipe books, mismatched bowls and archaic cooking utensils. I learnt a lot there and was always keen to get involved, whether it was scraping the earth from her home-grown new potatoes or stirring a saucepan of parsley sauce, I was there, sleeves rolled up and happy to help. Growing up as one of four children with as many pets in a tiny cottage, I treasured my solo visits to my grandparents' house — I would sit with them, shelling peas and slicing runner beans on the patio or sniffing the tomatoes in the greenhouse (it always seemed to be summer), it was a precious time and such a big part of my childhood.

Of course the highlight of my after-school visits usually centred around whatever sweet treats she had baked that day, her sticky flapjack was legendary and I still haven't tasted or been able to re-create a treacle tart superior to hers. She just seemed to have a knack of cooking simple things perfectly and as I've grown up I've realised more and more that that is not as easy as it seems.

At Christmas she would make her famous sherry trifle — it was a deliciously sloppy affair with no set custard or jelly allowed and it got boozier and boozier the older she got, as her eyesight deteriorated and her hand grew less steady. As a young girl it was a permitted taste of the forbidden and I savoured it just as I did the cherry brandy filled chocolates that also made an appearance at Christmas.

KIRSTIE ALLSOPP
TV Presenter

Where I was brought up in the country there were endless hedgerows and we always picked blackberries from them. About 14 years ago I really overdid things when making Location, Location, Location and I got a mild form of pneumonia. I took ten days off work and went to my parents' house in Dorset.

There was just me and my border terrier Foxy, so I began my recovery by watching the first three series of West Wing back to back. I also went on long walks and picked blackberries — loads of them — and made lots of lovely things, including blackberry vodka, blackberry jam and jelly, and blackberry and apple crumble.

These days, however, a family berry-picking expedition with the four boys means we rarely make it home with a single blackberry, so we end up eating apple crumble.

GET WELL SOON APPLE AND BLACKBERRY CRUMBLE

SERVES 6

Ingredients

700g COX'S APPLES,
cored and cut into wedges.

300g BLACKBERRIES.

JUICE of 1 ORANGE.

1 tsp GROUND MIXED SPICE.

2 tbsp LIGHT BROWN SOFT SUGAR

For the topping;

175g PLAIN FLOUR.

100g BUTTER, CHOPPED.

50g LIGHT BROWN SOFT SUGAR,
plus an extra tablespoon for sprinkling.

50g REGULAR ROLLED OATS.

Method

Preheat the oven to 200°C, 180°C fan, gas mark 6.

Put the apples in a bowl with the blackberries, orange juice, mixed spice and sugar.

Mix well then spoon into a shallow ovenproof dish.

To make the topping, put the flour into a large bowl and rub in the butter. Stir in the sugar and oats, then spoon the mixture over the fruit in a thin layer. Sprinkle the remaining tablespoon of sugar over the crumble.

Bake for 40 minutes, until the crumble is golden brown and the fruit underneath it has softened. Serve with custard.

JILLY COOPER CBE
Journalist and Author

I am so pleased to provide this recipe because my sweet friend Hazel, after suffering harrowing treatment for cancer, found her life transformed by ongoing visits to Maggie's and how glowingly she spoke of the comfort, fun and friendship they provided.

When we moved to Gloucestershire in 1982, I used to walk my dogs for hours around our lovely valley. Bewitched by the white blossom on the blackthorn bushes in the Spring, I discovered in the Autumn they were covered in purple berries known as sloes. Soon I was pausing for hours to pick them, to the disgust of my dogs who interpreted 'Sloe' as 'Slow' and got fed up hanging around.

Back home my evenings were spent pricking each berry to make sloe gin — the nicest after dinner drink on which to get merry!

Sadly, after a hip operation in 2015, I could no longer scour the valley to pick sloes so bought Gordon's Sloe Gin instead.

The following recipe for Fruit Salad is very haphazard, and quantities do vary, depending on how many people are to be catered for and what fruit is in season.

Stir all the fruit around until it is submerged.

Leave covered in the fridge for a few hours to marinate.

Serve with cream or enjoy in its Naked Glory!

DECADENT FRUIT SALAD

As a rough guide take:

ONE and A HALF PUNNETS of STRAWBERRIES, hulled and quartered.

ONE PUNNET of RASPBERRIES.

ONE PUNNET of BLUEBERRIES.

ANY BLACKBERRIES in season.

THIRTY SEEDLESS GREEN GRAPES, halved.

A QUARTER SLICE of any MELON, cut into nice chunks.

THREE RIPE NECTARINES, sliced from their stones.

TWO SATSUMAS, in individual segments.

TWENTY OR SO DRIED APRICOTS, halved.

TWO EATING APPLES, peeled, cored and diced.

TWO CONFERENCE PEARS, peeled, cored and diced.

and...

GORDON'S SLOE GIN

ROBINSON'S DOUBLE STRENGTH APPLE & BLACURRANT CORDIAL

Method

Pile all the fruit into a serving bowl, then cover with half to three quarters of a pint of Gordon's Sloe Gin.

Followed by half a pint of Robinson's double strength Blackcurrant & Apple cordial.

Add a teaspoon of sugar to taste.

Leave in the fridge overnight.

KATE PENNELL
Private Chef

Crème Brûlée is the most deliciously decadent dessert: the distinctive burnt toffee shell that shatters under the spoon to reveal a rich, velvety layer of vanilla custard. I am sharing my recipe because many people love it yet are afraid to give it a go. I can't imagine how confused the crème brûlée novice must be as there are so many variations of this classic that has a mere five ingredients.

This is my version, cooked and served many times for HRH The Prince of Wales. I am a crème brûlée purist, it's vanilla all the way for me, but I have a clear memory of being given the plumpest raspberries fresh from the Highgrove garden and, to this day, remember poking around in the scalding cream to get them to stay on the bottom and not float to the top.

SERVES SIX IN 125ml,
9cm DIAMETER RAMEKINS.

Ingredients

430ml DOUBLE CREAM.

100ml FULL FAT MILK.

5 LARGE EGG YOLKS.

2 VANILLA PODS.

50g CASTER SUGAR.

ROYAL CRÈME BRÛLÉE

Method

Put the egg yolks and the sugar in a bowl and whisk until slightly pale and creamy. I use a mixer but an electric hand whisk will do the job.

With a sharp knife, slit the vanilla pod open lengthways, scrape out the seeds and put the pod and the seeds into a pan with the milk and cream. Very gently bring almost to the boil – you will see bubbles begin to appear.
Just before boiling point, take the pan off the heat.

Remove the vanilla pod and then pour the vanilla-infused cream onto the beaten egg yolks, stirring with a whisk until combined. Strain through a fine sieve into a jug.
Give the mixture a stir and then, using a spoon, scoop off any foam that is sitting on top of the liquid.

Put the ramekins in a high sided roasting dish and divide the hot cream between them. Then pour cold water into the roasting tin so that it comes two-thirds of the way up the ramekins.

Place in an oven preheated to 150˚C, gas mark 2 and bake for about 35 minutes until the custard is set – they should wobble slightly when shaken. Don't let them get too firm. Lift out of the roasting dish and leave to cool – then refrigerate. They can be left overnight at this stage.

Remove your chilled ramekins from the fridge. Sprinkle a generous teaspoon of caster sugar over each custard and spread out with the back of a spoon to cover evenly and to the edges.

Now to caramelise the tops. I prefer to use a blowtorch, holding the flame just above the sugar and moving it around. The small crystals of caster sugar melt easily so you should be able to get an even, crisp caramel without charring. Don't rush this stage or you'll end up with an over-blackened brûlée.

It's possible to use a very hot grill instead of a blowtorch but if you do, make sure it's pre-heated and that the tops are as close to the heat source as possible.

You may need to move the ramekins around to ensure even caramelisation. Be careful not to warm up the custard so much that it cooks further.

Once coloured evenly, allow to cool, return the ramekins to the fridge until the sugar is hard, just 15 minutes or so should do it – then serve.

LEMON SOUFFLÉ

Ingredients

2 LEMONS, GRATED rind and juice.

2 LARGE EGGS.

5oz CASTER SUGAR.

3 tbsp COLD WATER.

2 tsp POWDERED GELATINE.

¼ pint DOUBLE CREAM.

ELIZABETH FLETCHER
Maggie's Oxford Volunteer

For many months after my husband's operation for oesophageal cancer, I needed to provide small, tasty meals with a high calorific value. One of his favourite desserts at this time was lemon soufflé, which I could freeze in ramekin dishes and thaw out individually whenever he wanted one.

This recipe reminds me of the challenging time during recovery and also to be thankful for his healthier diet now.

I hope you'll give it a go at home!

Method

Separate the egg yolks from the whites. Put lemon rind and juice, egg yolks and sugar into a basin over a pan of hot water. Whisk until thickened.

Dissolve the gelatine into the water using a small bowl heated by a pan of simmering water.

When the gelatine has dissolved, stir it into the lemon mixture and leave in a cool place until just beginning to set.

Whisk the cream to soft peaks and fold into the lemon mixture.

Using a clean whisk, beat the egg whites stiffly, then fold into the mixture.

Turn the mixture into individual ramekin dishes and leave in a cool place to set.

Cover the ramekins and freeze.

Remove the ramekins from the freezer as required.

Serve with mixed fruit.

DAWN RAND
Maggie's Cambridge Volunteer

I've always enjoyed cooking from a very young age. I developed a real passion for baking when I started my nurse training 32 years ago. I remember testing recipes on my friends and colleagues, and creating cakes at very odd hours to share and reflect on our day. I guess baking to me is therapeutic and sharing a cake is the simplest way to show you care.

At Maggie's, I find bringing a cake and discussing the recipe helps to form a connection with visitors around the table. It can open a conversation and start a discussion within a group or one to one. I often experiment, trying out sugar free and gluten free recipes, for example.

For this book, I took some cakes into the Centre and this was voted the best. It's not the healthiest but is gluten free. I adapted the recipe from one given to me by a very dear friend. It's best enjoyed on a warm summer's evening sitting with friends or family with pistachio nuts sprinkled on top, and extra raspberries and cream. Though my son likes to have melted chocolate on his!

SPICED ORANGE AND ALMOND TORTE

Ingredients

1 MEDIUM SIZED ORANGE.

10 RASPBERRIES.

3 EGGS.

180g GOLDEN CASTER SUGAR.

250g GROUND ALMONDS.

½ tsp BAKING POWDER.

½ tsp POWDERED GINGER.

½ tsp MIXED SPICE.

¼ tsp ALLSPICE.

PINCH OF SALT.

Method

Put the whole orange in a small saucepan, cover with water and bring to the boil. Simmer for an hour until soft, then remove and leave to cool. Once cool cut in half, remove the pips, and puree in a food processor.

Place sugar and eggs in a bowl and whisk until pale and thick. Then fold in the orange puree, ground almonds, baking powder and spices. Lastly, gently fold in the raspberries.

Pour the mix into a greased and lined 20cm spring-form baking tin. Bake in the oven for 45 minutes at 180°C, fan 160°C, gas mark 4. Once cooked, allow the cake to cool in the tin.

I recommend serving with chopped pistachios and cream!

BEN SHIRES
TV Presenter

The thing about heading off to university for the first time as a confident and cocksure 18 year-old is, despite the unshakeable belief that you know absolutely everything, it soon becomes painfully clear that you know absolutely nothing.

The biggest gaps in my knowledge were to be found in the culinary department, and thus, after a particularly humbling incident involving a badly burnt omelette and a disgruntled fire brigade, I sought words of comfort and wisdom from the most accomplished chef I knew: Mum.

Having galvanised me with a rundown of the kitchen basics, she also entrusted me, carefully and conspiratorially, with this, her deceptively simple banana bread showstopper – the famed family favourite made with the help of a legendary recipe, shrouded in secrecy.

As it turned out, the secret was she'd been using an old Bero cookbook the whole time. Still, it always went down a storm whenever I made it in my (newly-refurbished) uni halls, and it kick-started my love affair with cookery shortcuts; a lesson I look forward to passing on to my own kids one day.

LEGENDARY BANANA LOAF

Ingredients

225g (8oz) SELF RAISING FLOUR.

¼ tsp BICARBONATE OF SODA.

PINCH OF SALT.

75g (3oz) BUTTER.

175g (6oz) CASTER SUGAR.

2 MEDIUM EGGS, BEATEN.

450g (1lb) BANANAS, PEELED AND MASHED (weighed before peeling).

100g (4oz) WALNUTS, CHOPPED.

Method

Heat oven to 180°C, 350°F, gas mark 4. Grease the base of a 1kg (2lb) loaf tin and line with foil, leaving excess hanging over the edge to allow for subsequent easy extraction.

Mix together flour, bicarbonate of soda and salt.

Cream the butter and sugar until pale and fluffy.
Add the eggs a little at a time alternately with the flour.

Stir in the remaining flour, bananas and walnuts and place in the pre-prepared tin. Cover loosely with foil to prevent burning and bake for about 75 minutes.

Cool on a wire rack.

Devour unceremoniously.

JEREMY VINE
TV and Radio Presenter

When I first lived in London on my own in the late eighties, I would throw dinner parties and try to make them as extravagant as possible. My thought was that I could show off incredible cooking skills to friends. The one flaw was that I really couldn't cook (there was a particularly unfortunate incident with some mussels, I remember) and my home — an ex-council house in Northolt — was as unglamorous as you can possibly imagine. But this recipe makes you look like a Michelin-starred chef without needing any skill at all. Leaving aside the fire risk, it is a winner. It will be the talk of Northolt if you try it.

EXTRAVAGANT FLAMBÉED BANANAS

Ingredients and Method

Heat a cup of decent red wine. As it warms, introduce a tsp of grated orange rind and a pinch of grated lemon rind. Then add half a cup of brown sugar, and spices in the following quantities: a pinch of ground cloves, $\frac{1}{2}$ a tsp of nutmeg and the same quantity of cinnamon.

Peel 5 ripe bananas and sprinkle them with lemon juice (which stops them going brown). Put them in your syrup and gradually warm them, turning them so they soak really nicely.

Now the dramatic bit. Sprinkle the bananas with chopped almonds, pour a good quantity of rum over them and set the bananas alight. Under low lighting take the pan straight to the table and serve your bananas with ice cream and lashings of your beautiful red syrup.

WELSH APPLE CAKE

Ingredients

APPLE MIX:

1lb EATING APPLES,
peeled, cored and diced into 1cm pieces.

2oz SULTANAS.

1oz WALNUTS.

½ tsp GROUND CINNAMON.

2oz DEMERARA SUGAR (consider leaving
out or sprinkling on top for crunch).

CAKE BATTER:

4oz CASTER SUGAR.

5oz SELF RAISING FLOUR.

4oz MELTED BUTTER.

1 LARGE EGG.

Method

Stir all the apple mix ingredients together.

Combine the cake batter ingredients and beat. Spread two thirds of the batter into a lined eight inch round tin or square seven inch tin.

Cover with apple mix then spoon the remaining batter on top. Make sure the edges are covered but the apple mix can be exposed in other areas. Push down the sultanas.

Bake at 180°C, fan 170°C for 50–60 minutes until well risen and springy.

Serve cold in little squares or warm with custard.

JOANNA GROVE-LAFARGE
Maggie's Supporter

I bought my cottage from a gentleman who found out he had terminal cancer just as we completed the sale. He died a few weeks afterwards.

He was an amazing man. An accomplished skier and rugby player he was a geography and PE teacher at a local boys' school, taking the boys on sporting trips abroad throughout the 60s and 70s. When he retired he took up painting and his work was displayed in galleries and sold. He was also a self-taught carpenter and used these skills in and around the cottage.

We had become friends and I have several memories from my visits during the sale: him asking me exactly which vegetables I liked and making sure he planted those; walking round the garden with him as he told me in great detail about the fruit trees; and his skill in creating recipes from the produce available to him that very day in the garden. His wife had died from cancer eight years previously and he had taught himself to cook so the recipes were always interesting.

There are three knarled trees in the garden that produce amazing apples and this recipe is one my friend used to make the most of the fruit. It's a winner every time.

NICHOLAS ALLAN
Author and Illustrator
of Best Selling
Childrens' Picture Books

At midday or afternoon my father put on his trunks, and, barefooted, leapt across the main road, down the long flight of stone steps, across the marine road, across the pebbled beach, and dived straight into the blue or green or battleship grey Brighton sea. Forty minutes later, he took exactly the same path back and arrived home bone dry. There, a cup of Blue Mountain coffee from a Turkish copper pot, blended with hot milk, and a heavy axe head of Slabkuchen lay ready waiting on the table. And that's when I and my brothers had some too, often warm, straight from the bread tin. Sometimes he'd break off a chunk, like a piece from a French stick, if the appropriate cutlery wasn't immediately to hand.

My father remained fit all his life because, of course, of the swims, and despite, of course, of the Slabkuchen. My mother remained fit all her life looking after my father.

Ingredients

1 tsp BAKING SODA.

1 cup of SOUR CREAM.

As many GLAZED CHERRIES as the cake can accommodate.

SLABKUCHEN

2 cups of ALL-PURPOSE FLOUR

1 cup of cut-up WALNUTS.

½ cup of GROUND ALMONDS.

1 cup of SUGAR.

1 EGG.

1 tsp of SALT.

2 cups of RAISINS.

Method

Take a 9 by 5 inch bread tin and line it with greased baking paper.

Mix the baking soda and sour cream together, throw in the fruit and nuts, mix, and then add everything else. Pour it all into the tin.

Place the tin in an oven preheated to 325°F and cook for about 1½ hours. Keep going until you see the crust getting as dark as you think you can take it, or at risk of incineration.

My mother learned that a minimum of two cakes should be baked for a week's consumption.

ROB REES, MBE DL
Global Entrepreneur

For most people Christmas is a special time of the year full of glorious smells, tastes and traditions. For me though, the Christmas Pudding means so much more as it's my earliest memory of cooking. Inspired by both my mother and my Nana, I can recall (aged 4) donning an apron that hung from head to toe and being lifted high on a stool to help weigh, mix and stir the freshest of homemade Christmas Puddings.

Each year the same large bowl would come out from my Nan's cupboard and be dusted off. At the same time a well thumbed early 1900s recipe book would come out with the weights and measures of the ingredients — plump sultanas, currants and raisins, homemade glazed fruits, butcher-purchased suet and freshly made breadcrumbs from the Co-op, which I recall in the days when 'Co-op Stamps' were a valid actual thing!

We grated carrots, potatoes and apples and softened the mix with beaten eggs, lots of sticky black treacle and Guinness — designed, as my Nan would say then, 'to put hairs on my chest'. Made each year on Stir-Up Sunday after a 24-hour soaking, each family member would come and stir the mix, make a wish and pay homage to 'The Pud'. We would make at least a dozen puddings each year for the extended family as gifts and each one would have a secret ingredient added as well as a good old-fashioned sixpence for the surprise winner of a full year's good luck on Christmas Day.

MEMORIES OF CHRISTMAS PUDDING

Ingredients

125g local SELF-RAISING FLOUR.

250g artisan WHITE BREADCRUMBS.

250g SUET.

250g DARK BROWN SUGAR.

1 tsp ALLSPICE.

150g CURRANTS. 300g RAISINS.

150g SULTANAS. 75g MIXED PEEL.

25g GROUND ALMONDS.

Grated rind of 1 LEMON.

¼ grated NUTMEG.

4 'Cotswold Legbar' or other local EGGS.

1 tbsp BLACK TREACLE.

Juice of 1 ORANGE.

½ grated CARROT.

½ grated COOKING APPLE.

1 CAN of GUINNESS or bottle of Ale or other local beer!

Method

Mix all ingredients together in large bowl and allow to soak overnight. Note: when adding the alcohol only add enough to create a mixture that is of 'dropping consistency' — that's when the mixture drops steadily off your spoon into the bowl. But remember that the dried fruit will soak up some of the liquid overnight so it doesn't matter too much if the mixture is a little wet.

Place the mix into a buttered pudding basin, filling it to an inch from the top. Cut buttered greaseproof paper to fit the top, wrap in either muslin or tin foil and tie ready for steaming.

Steam for 10 hours. Re-heat on Christmas day by steaming for a further 2 hours. The key to a dark, moist and rich pudding is in the steaming — the longer you can do it the better it becomes.

CHOCOLATE DENVER PUDDING

Ingredients

¾ cup SUGAR.

¾ cup FLOUR.

2 tsp BAKING POWDER.

A pinch of SALT.

1oz CHOCOLATE or 3 tbsp COCOA.

2lbs BUTTER.

½ cup MILK.

½ tsp VANILLA.

Ingredients

½ cup BROWN SUGAR.

½ cup WHITE SUGAR.

4 tbsp COCOA.

1½ cups COLD WATER or COFFEE.

Method

Sift sugar, flour, baking powder and salt. Add the chocolate and butter, melted. Add the milk and vanilla. Pour into a buttered dish. Over the top scatter brown and white sugar and cocoa. Pour over the cold water and coffee.

Bake for 40 minutes at 180°C, 350°F.
Let it stand at room temperature.

Serve with cream or ice cream (it needs this because it is, admittedly, rather a rich pudding, what with one thing and another, and the cream takes the edge off that richness).

CRESSIDA COWELL
Writer and Illustrator of
The How to Train Your Dragon
and *Wizards of Once* Series.

Although I grew up in London, where my father worked, we spent every summer on a tiny, uninhabited island off the west coast of Scotland. The island had no roads, houses or electricity, it was just a storm-blown wilderness of sea-birds and heather — but the perfect place to stimulate a child's imagination.

This is a recipe for Chocolate Denver Pudding, crispy on the top, gooey in the middle, chocolatey all the way through, and just the kind of food you wanted to eat when you had spent a wet and windy day outside on the island. I've included a photo of the recipe in my mother's handwriting. My mother was a great friend of Maggie Keswick Jencks, the founder of Maggie's Centres.

Ingredients

125g UNSALTED BUTTER, melted.

175g PLAIN FLOUR.

150g CASTER SUGAR.

2 LARGE EGGS.

1 tsp VANILLA EXTRACT.

4 SMALL RIPE BANANAS, mashed
(they can be brown).

100g DARK CHOCOLATE chopped
into chunks or a packet of chocolate chunks.

2 tsp BAKING POWDER.

½ tsp BICARBONATE of SODA.

½ tsp SALT

GEORGIA THOMAS
Teen Cookbook Author
and YouTuber

This is one of the first recipes I ever made with my mum (from a Nigella Lawson recipe), and me and my brothers love it so much, we never tire of it, no matter how many times we make it. I remember at the age of about 12 feeling quite proud of myself the first time I made it without any help. It was this realisation that I could create that utterly delicious loaf myself — and as long as I had clear instructions and all the ingredients, there was nothing stopping me cooking other things too. It was quite empowering.

When I came to start cooking for my Duke of Edinburgh award though, I didn't always find it easy because often the instructions in cookbooks assume a lot of knowledge (you'd be surprised how many teenagers don't know what 'tbsp' means). So when I was trying to think of ideas to raise funds to go on a school expedition, my mum and I decided to create a cookbook for teens. We included basic recipes which would be useful for those going away to college, family meals, bakes such as this one and the sort of food teenagers like to eat with their mates. It's called *50 Recipes Teenagers Can Tackle* and it's proved very popular with parents and teenagers alike!

But this one is my all-time favourite, in my view, the ultimate comfort bake. It's best eaten with custard, about 15 to 30 minutes after it's come out of the oven, when it will still be hot in the middle and crunchy on the outside.

CHOCOLATE AND BANANA LOAF

THIS RECIPE SERVES 8.

PREPARATION TIME IS 20 MINUTES WITH START TO FINISH TIME OF 1 HOUR 20 MINUTES.

YOU'LL NEED A MIXING BOWL, LOAF TIN AND LOAF TIN LINER.

Method

Preheat your oven to 170°C, gas mark 3 and set the shelf at just below the middle postion. Line the loaf tin with a loaf tin liner or, if you don't have one, grease with butter and dust with flour.

Using a glass bowl, melt the butter in the microwave on a low setting. Put the melted butter into a mixing bowl with the sugar and whisk together. Beat the eggs into the mixture and add the vanilla. Mash the bananas on a plate and add them into the mixture. Then add the chocolate chunks.

Weigh out the flour into your weighing scale bowl and into that bowl add the baking powder, bicarbonate of soda and salt. Mix it around gently. Then gradually add the flour mixture into the mixing bowl, stirring in after each addition.

Tip and scrape the contents of your bowl into the lined or greased loaf tin. Place the tin into the middle of the preheated oven and set your timer for 1 hour.

As you come towards the end of the cooking time, keep an eye on the cake to make sure it's not starting to burn on the top (ideally without opening the oven door as that could make it sink). If it looks like it could burn, turn the oven down to around 150°C.

After cooking, leave the cake to cool as it will be easier to cut and serve. We like custard with ours but it's gorgeous on its own too!

DEE CAMPLING
Interior Stylist

This is a recipe that my mum always makes and now I make it and so do my children. The large portion of beetroot in it makes you feel like you're eating something really healthy and, in our minds, offsets the large portion of dark chocolate that's also in the cake!

My mum has always made cakes for us — food is her way of nurturing I think — and sitting around as a family, chatting over a large slab of cake and a cup of tea is one of the simplest and best pleasures in life.

My mum recently adapted this recipe when I took up a vegan diet, and it's just as delicious.

(VEGAN) CHOCOLATE CAKE

Ingredients

50g (2oz) COCOA POWDER.

175g (6oz) PLAIN FLOUR.

1½ tsp BAKING POWDER.

200g (7oz) CASTER SUGAR.

250g pack of BEETROOT.

3 MEDIUM EGGS or for a VEGAN VERSION 200ml NON-DAIRY MILK.

200ml (7floz) SUNFLOWER OIL.

100g (3½oz) DARK CHOCOLATE finely chopped.

ICING SUGAR to serve.

Method

Preheat the oven to 180°C, fan 160°C, gas mark 4, then grease and line the bottom of a 23cm (8½ to 9 inch) loose-bottomed cake tin.

Sieve the flour, cocoa powder and sugar into a large bowl.

Drain and halve the beetroot, then blend in a food processor. With the machine running, add the eggs one at a time then pour in the oil. Blend the mixture till the liquid is just smooth.

Stir the wet mixture into the dry ingredients and mix in the chocolate. Pour into the tin and cook for 45 minutes until a skewer comes out clean.

Remove from the oven and set aside for 10 minutes, then turn out and leave to cool.

Dust the cake with icing sugar just before serving.

CHOCOLATE CRUNCH

Ingredients and Method

Well grease a Swiss roll size tin.

In a bowl put 340g of porridge oats and 80g of soft brown sugar. In a pan slowly melt 170g of butter, then stir in a good heaped tablespoon of golden syrup. Mix well into the dry ingredients.

Spread into the tin and bake in a moderate oven at 180°C for about 30 mins or until it looks cooked! It should be lightly brown and firm but still soft to the touch. Better to be slightly soft than too hard.

Whilst the crunch is in the oven, make up a quantity of basic chocolate glace icing: sifted icing sugar and a little cocoa powder (depending on how strong you want it), mixed with hot water. The consistency should be thick but not so thick that you cannot pour it.

As soon as the mixture comes out of the oven, pour over the warm chocolate glace icing straight away so that it seeps into the crunch.

Cut into squares once cold.

RACHEL TREWEEK
Bishop of Gloucester,
The Right Rev.d

This was a very popular recipe in our family when I was a child. I have no idea where the original recipe came from but this lovely chocolatey, oaty slice was a regular filling in our cake tins, and those of my grandma and aunts.

My Mum was a skilled and avid baker and this quick and simple recipe brings back warm memories of our home in Broxbourne, Hertfordshire, which was a place where friends of all ages were welcome. No doubt, my Mum's thinking behind her weekly baking was one of managing the pennies with a young family, so the cake tins were usually full with a fairly standard array of biscuits and cakes, which I confess at times I found rather repetitive.

However, my friends loved coming to our home and consuming my Mum's home-baked fare. I, on the other hand, rather enjoyed going to homes where factory-made cakes were on offer, although I was frequently disappointed as in the 1960s and 70s the wrapping and colour of such cakes were often more attractive than the actual taste and texture.

On reflection, I wonder if this delicious recipe added to my love of chocolate and cake, both of which now seem to be part of my staple diet!

NELL GIFFORD
Giffords Circus Producer and Owner

Cuban circus strongman Juan Ozniel Posso Pita came into my life last summer. Formidably strong and yet with the unmistakable Cuban rhythm and musicality 'Posso' has charmed everyone with his flashing gold smile and determinedly cheerful outlook. Like many Cubans he has a forbiddingly sweet tooth and is a great cook. Posso has been my constant support and tower of strength throughout my treatment as I recover from cancer, a real-life strongman!

My big sister Emma Bridgewater had the genius idea of creating a special 'Strongman Cake' especially for this cookbook and our Circus Sauce head chef Ols Halas has devised this rich chocolatey recipe, which is best eaten with strong tea, or for the full Cuban effect, hot milk with sugar stirred into it. Strong, zesty and powerful, it's the perfect afternoon tea pick-me-up!

Ingredients

250g COCONUT YOGHURT.

125g CASTER SUGAR.

220g FLOUR.

250g SUGAR.

125ml VEGETABLE OIL.

STRONGMAN CAKE

2 LIMES, zest and juice.

1 tsp GROUND GINGER.

2 tsp BAKING POWDER.

3 EGGS.

1 tsp VANILLA EXTRACT.

20g COCOA POWDER.

PINCH of SALT.

ICING:

250g CREAM CHEESE.

200ml DULCH DE LECHE (cooked condensed milk).

1 SHOT of DARK SPICED RUM.

COCOA POWDER to dust.

Method

Very simply, mix all the ingredients for the cake together in a large bowl or mixer and pour into a lined round 6-inch baking tin.

Bake at 160°C for 30–40 minutes then prod a skewer in the centre and ensure it's clean when pulled out.

Remove the cake from the tin and leave on a cooling rack to rest.

In a mixer, begin beating the cream cheese with the whisk attachment then add the rum and dulce de leche (which is a Latin American delicacy of cooked sweetened milk).

Slice the cake in half and spoon the mix on with a pallet knife, in the middle of the sandwich and all over.

With a piping bag, form spikes on the top and dust with cocoa powder.

If you're adventurous, make some shiny dumbells to crown your creation!

Ingredients

FOR THE CAKE:

COOKING SPRAY.

1 cup (250ml) UNSWEETENED COCOA
POWDER (Natural or Dutch Process).

2½ cups (625ml) ALL-PURPOSE FLOUR.

2 cups (500ml) SUGAR.

1½ tsp (7ml) BAKING POWDER.

1 tsp (5ml) BAKING SODA.

1 tsp (5ml) SALT.

3 LARGE EGGS, room temperature.

¾ cup (175ml) CANOLA OIL.

½ cup (125ml) SOUR CREAM.

2 tsp (10ml) VANILLA.

½ cup (125ml) ORANGE MARMALADE.

FOR THE ICING:

2 cups (500ml) 35% WHIPPING CREAM.

½ cup (125ml) SUGAR.

1/3 cup (75ml) COCOA, sifted.

FOR THE CARAMEL:

½ cup (125ml) SUGAR.

1 tbsp (15ml) CORN SYRUP.

½ cup (125ml) 35% WHIPPING CREAM.

1 tbsp (15ml) UNSALTED BUTTER.

½ tsp (2ml) KOSHER SALT
or FLAKED SEA SALT.

YORKSHIRE ROWS

FRANCES DAVIES, NIKI DOEG, HELEN BUTTERS, JANETTE BENADDI.

4 Ordinary Extraordinary Mums Who Rowed Across The Atlantic.

On the boat we had carefully stashed away a single chocolate orange for Christmas which we were saving and intending to share equally. However, in the midst of a hurricane, Frances and Janette decided they would eat it. Not only did they eat it all, they filmed themselves eating it — adding insult to injury! So chocolate oranges are actually quite a sore point with certain members of the team. But we would have loved to have eaten this wonderful cake on the boat — shared equally of course!

DARK CHOCOLATE ORANGE CAKE WITH SEA SALTED CARAMEL

Method

Preheat oven to 350°F (180°C). Coat two 9-inch (22cm) round pans with cooking spray and line the bottoms with parchment paper.

Whisk cocoa with 1½ cups (375ml) boiling water in a medium bowl until smooth. Set aside.

In a large mixing bowl, whisk flour, sugar, baking powder, soda and salt until well combined.

Add eggs, canola oil, sour cream and vanilla. Beat with a mixer on medium speed for about 1 minute until smooth.

Reduce the mixer speed to low and add cocoa mixture in a slow stream until just combined. Scrape down sides and give a few turns with a spatula. The batter will be thin. Divide the batter between the pans, tapping on the counter to release any bubbles.

Bake for 30 to 40 minutes until a toothpick inserted in the centre comes out clean. Cool on racks.

To assemble, slice each layer in half to make 4 layers. Place 1 layer on a cake plate and spread with 2 tbsp (30ml) of orange marmalade. Repeat with the other layers.

Cover the whole cake with chocolate whipped cream frosting and drizzle with salted caramel (recipes below).

CHOCOLATE WHIPPED CREAM ICING

In a small mixing bowl, combine 2 cups (500ml) of 35% whipping cream, ½ a cup (125ml) of sugar and 1/3 cup (75 ml) of sifted cocoa. Chill for 15 minutes, then beat until stiff peaks form.

SALTED CARAMEL

Bring ½ a cup (125ml) of sugar and 1 tbsp (15ml) of corn syrup to a simmer over medium heat in a small saucepan.

Cook, swirling the pan, not stirring, until the mixture becomes amber. This will take about 4 minutes. Remove from the heat and carefully whisk in ½ a cup (125ml) of 35% whipping cream and 1 tbsp (15ml) of unsalted butter until smooth.

Add a pinch to ½ tsp (2ml) of flaked sea salt or kosher salt to taste. Cool for 10–15 minutes. If you don't want to go to the trouble of making your own caramel, store-bought works great. Just warm in the microwave for 20 seconds and add the salt.

GREAT AUNT FLO'S BIRTHDAY TIFFIN

Ingredients

100g BUTTER.

150g GOLDEN SYRUP.

250g PLAIN BISCUITS
Particularly Digestives.

300g CHOCOLATE, a combination
of dark and milk as preferred.

JO CARTLEDGE
Maggie's Nottingham Volunteer

When I first volunteered at Maggie's Nottingham, I found a
tin with broken biscuits in the kitchen. These were going to
be discarded as they couldn't be offered to visitors. I took
them home and made the Tiffin recipe. That was six years
ago and by popular request I still bring Tiffin to Maggie's
every time I come in to volunteer!

The recipe came from my Great Aunt Flo. When I was a
little girl she gave me a special cake on my birthday every
year. In those days she called it American Chocolate Cake
and I had never tasted anything so delicious before!
This has developed into the Tiffin recipe I use today.

Method

Line an 18cm square loose based tin with cling film.

In a pan melt butter, chocolate broken into squares
and golden syrup very gently, so that the chocolate
does not overheat.

Crush the biscuits into small, bite sized pieces in a
large bowl.

When the chocolate mixture has melted, pour onto
the broken biscuits and stir until the biscuits are
all covered.

Tip the mixture into the prepared tin, level the
surface, then put into the fridge until it has cooled
and set, ideally overnight.

Turn out and cut into squares.

Chocolate Nancy will keep well for up to two weeks if put in an airtight container in a cool place.

LISA SMITH
Ginger Bakers — Head Ginger

This started as my reproduction of the bake that my Grandma made for me when I had left home and was going back to University. It was my piece of home and my connection to my Grandma. I named it Ella's treat; she was and remains an enormous inspiration, a strong independent woman with an entrepreneurial spirit.

After a recipe update and a desire to continue the family connection I developed Chocolate Nancy. Nancy is my daughter and, despite never meeting, these two important females in my life are forever connected. Unique to Ginger Bakers, this is an eye-catching, cheeky oat bar crammed with fruit and nut goodness and topped with a smothering of plain chocolate. You can be creative and exchange any of the fruits and nuts for those of your choice and create a unique bar of your own. A cornerstone of the Ginger Bakers collection with a history all of it's own.

Ingredients

220ml sweetened CONDENSED MILK.

150g salted BUTTER.

1 tbsp finely grated LEMON ZEST.

170g JUMBO OATS (gluten free if you prefer).

140g DRIED CRANBERRIES.

120g DRIED APRICOTS chopped finely.

CHOCOLATE NANCY

120g SULTANAS. 60g DESICCATED COCONUT.

60g whole BLANCHED ALMONDS chopped.

60g shelled PISTACHIOS chopped.

FOR THE TOPPING:

100g good quality PLAIN CHOCOLATE

60g salted BUTTER

DRIED CRANBERRIES and PISTACHIOS chopped finely.

Method

Line a tray bake tin (approximately 23cm by 23cm) with baking parchment so that it covers the base and the sides. Melt the butter and the condensed milk in a pan over a gentle heat until the two are well combined. Stir the mixture continuously making sure it doesn't burn. Set aside to cool slightly. Measure out all the dry ingredients into a large bowl and give them a good stir folding them over so they are all evenly combined. Pour over the melted butter and condensed milk mixture and mix well. The mixture should be slightly sticky.

Pour the mixture into the lined tin. Spread it evenly, pushing it into the corners and making sure it's pressed well and is flat and smooth on top. Chill in the fridge for about 30 minutes. You may want to help the pressing by placing another piece of baking parchment on top of the mixture and putting a weight on top. This could be something like a small stack of books, or another tray with a bag of sugar on it. In the meantime, you can prepare the topping. Finely chop a handful of dried cranberries and shelled pistachios and set aside.

The chocolate topping can be made either in a Bain Marie or in the microwave. Either way, make sure you don't overheat the chocolate, which results in it appearing dull and without its attractive shine. Place the butter and chocolate in a microwavable bowl, heat for 30 seconds at a time, stirring well between each heating until both are melted and well combined. Take the chilled base mixture out of the refrigerator and pour the chocolate mixture over the top, tilting the tray from side to side until it is completely covered. Sprinkle with the cranberries and pistachios before the chocolate sets. Allow the topping to set completely, then cut into your preferred size pieces and serve.

123

MAGGIE KESWICK JENCKS

ABOUT MAGGIE'S

Maggie's is a charity that provides free cancer support and information in centres across the UK and online.

In 1996, we created a place for anyone who is living with cancer and their family and friends, in the grounds of an NHS hospital in Edinburgh. We named the centre after our inspirational founder, Maggie.

Maggie lived with advanced cancer for two years and used her experiences to create a blueprint for a new type of care. Her belief that "above all, what matters is not to lose the joy of living in the fear of dying" has informed everything at our centres, from the beautiful architecture and choice of artwork to the relaxed, welcoming layouts and our warm friendly approach.

Today you will find Maggie's across the UK and even abroad. Each of our 22 centres is staffed by an expert team, including support specialists, psychologists and benefits advisors. They are places to find practical advice about benefits and eating well; for emotional support; to share experiences with others in a similar situation around the kitchen table or in our online community; or just to sit quietly with a cup of tea.

Our unique programme of support has been shown to strengthen the physical and emotional well-being of people living with cancer and their family and friends.

To find out more, or to find your nearest Maggie's, please visit www.maggiescentres.org

"MAGGIE'S PROVIDED ME WITH A REFUGE — A SANCTUARY."

"MAGGIE'S PROVIDED ME WITH A REFUGE — PART OF THE REAL WORLD BUT SOMEHOW DETACHED. THE WORLD HADN'T CHANGED BUT CANCER HAD TOTALLY CHANGED WHO I WAS AND I NEEDED HELP TO LEARN HOW TO LIVE AGAIN."

ISOBEL, MAGGIE'S VISITOR

MAGGIE'S CENTRES

EDINBURGH

GLASGOW

DUNDEE

HIGHLANDS

FIFE

FORTH VALLEY

LANARKSHIRE

ABERDEEN

NEWCASTLE

MANCHESTER

NOTTINGHAM

SWANSEA

MERSEYSIDE (INTERIM CENTRE)

OLDHAM

CHELTENHAM

OXFORD

WEST LONDON

BARTS

CAMBRIDGE (INTERIM CENTRE)

ROYAL FREE (INTERIM CENTRE)

TOKYO

HONG KONG

FUTURE CENTRES:

ROYAL MARSDEN

CARDIFF

LEEDS

SOUTHAMPTON

NORTHAMPTON

TAUNTON

BARCELONA (KALIDA)

MAGGIE'S ONLINE

Maggie's Online Centre is available 24 hours a day, all year round. It is staffed Monday to Friday 9am–5pm.

WWW.MAGGIESCENTRES.ORG

NATASHA WILLMORE · CULPEPPER & CO

We lost my stepfather, Roger Franklin, to leukaemia a few years ago. Some of his treatment took place in Bristol and when he was there my mum and I travelled from the Cotswolds to visit him several times a week. Before making the long journey home, we would order a 'Pastel de Nata' and a cuppa at a little food stall in St Nicholas Market. Just the sight of this little treat takes me back to those days, and the enormous pride we had in Roger's bravery and strength.

My mum and Roger could really have benefited from Maggie's. He was an artist, a highly creative man who needed an inspirational environment and somewhere to talk through the many concerns that effect everyone touched by cancer.

Sadly, we didn't know about Maggie's until after our wonderful Roger passed away. But when I found out more, I took my mum along to the Cheltenham centre, and she had the most amazing support. You feel welcome and at peace the minute you step through the door. The big kitchen table with a cup of tea and cake is like coming home. It's a very special place.

KELLY JAMES · SHADOWPLAY DESIGN

When I was growing up my Nanny used to be a big part of my life and I have many memories of happy times spent at my grandparents' house. Nanny and Gramp would always have a Sunday roast and, as a youngster I would go there for lunch with my parents. But even when I left home I would be cheeky and just turn up, as would assorted cousins, uncles and aunts. We'd all just drop in around lunchtime knowing a roast would be almost ready — what a bunch of chancers we were!

Luckily, Nanny and Gramp loved having a full house and there was always enough for everybody. The beef was always slow-cooked so it was as soft as the vegetables — which, in accord with the practice of the time, were well-boiled. The roast potatoes were my favourite. Cooked in beef dripping saved from the previous week, they were delicious. I would have been more than satisfied with just a plate of roasties!

My old Gramp died of lung cancer and my lovely Nanny has dementia and is now being cared for. My mum visits her every day but brings her home for a roast every Sunday, so the story goes on...

PHIL JAMES · SHADOWPLAY

My mum had four children including me, and as well as working full-time she also cared for our disabled grandmother. To make life even more complicated, my dad worked night shifts. All this meant careful food planning was an absolute must and mum organised every day so we knew exactly what we were eating.

Thursday was supermarket shopping day and we had always had 'Burgers in Baps' for tea. There was an extra incentive too. If I helped with the food shopping, I was given a bag of Opal Fruits as a treat, and I used to eat the whole bag while watching *Top of the Pops*!

These memories stick. Even now, I still think of Thursdays as 'Burgers in Baps Day'.

SAVOURY

SWEET

A BIG THANK YOU

Peter Carnell — Our amazing editor
and copywriter

OTHER BAKERS & MAKERS:

Sue Everson

Iain Girdlestone

Kate Pennell

Mary Davey

Sue Dudfield

Jax Franklin

Flora Mountford

Dee Campling

Georgia Thomas

Maria Pascoe

Oliver Halas — Head Chef
Giffords Circus Sauce

HELPERS:

Mike Anderson — Emotive New Media

Sue Everson

Ryan Riley

David Orme

Kieran Wakefield

Catherine Smith

Max Sawyer

Martha Peace

Maisie Willmore

Jess Cook — Silverball PR

Emma Luther — Silverball PR

Cate Hamilton

Cooper & Jackson James

SUPPORTERS:

Shadowplay Design

Shadowplay Media

Culpepper & Company

Cheltenham Literature Festival

Tewkesbury Printing Company

The Find, Cheltenham

Anna Mason — Maggie's Cheltenham

Catherine & Richard Scudamore

Anna Jones — Cotswold Connections

Alastair Bennett — Premier League

Wendy Preston — Love Food Marketing

Carly Appleby

Carey White — @mylegoman

Angela & Dave Higgins

Mark Willmore

Beryl & Ivor Willmore

PHOTO CREDITS:

Photography — Phil James, Shadowplay

Michael Perry (portrait) —
Anderson & Bergdahl Photography

Jilly Cooper (portrait) —
Edward Whitaker, Racing Post

Kirstie Allsopp (portrait) —
Fiona Murray

Martha Kearney (portrait) —
David Montgomery

All centre images supplied by Maggie's

THE CREATIVE TEAM:

who have donated their time to create this cookbook

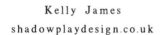

Kelly James
shadowplaydesign.co.uk

Natasha Willmore
culpepperandcompany.co.uk

·SHADOWPLAY·®

Photography by Phil James
shadowplay.co.uk

OUR SPONSORS

unicorn HOUSE

QUICKGRIND
carbide tooling

THE FIND

COOK
Cheltenham

RAVENHURST
Luxury Bed & Breakfast